Taking Hypnosis to the Next Level:

Valuable Tips for Enhancing Your Clinical Practice

by

Michael D. Yapko, PhD

Also by Michael D. Yapko, PhD

The Discriminating Therapist: Asking "How" Questions, Making Distinctions, and Finding Direction in Therapy. Fallbrook, CA.: Yapko Publications, 2016.

Keys to Unlocking Depression: An Internationally Known Depression Expert Tells You What You Need to Know to Overcome Depression.
Fallbrook, CA.: Yapko Publications, 2016.

Essentials of Hypnosis, 2nd edition. New York: Routledge, 2015.

Trancework: An Introduction to the Practice of Clinical Hypnosis, 4th edition. New York: Routledge, 2012.

Mindfulness and Hypnosis: The Power of Suggestion to Transform Experience. New York: Norton, 2011.

Depression is Contagious: How the Most Common Mood Disorder is Spreading Around the World and How to Stop It. New York: The Free Press, 2009.

Hypnosis and Treating Depression: Applications in Clinical Practice (Editor). New York: Routledge, 2006.

Treating Depression with Hypnosis: Integrating Cognitive-Behavioral and Strategic Approaches. New York: Brunner/Routledge, 2001.

Hand-Me-Down Blues: How to Stop Depression from Spreading in Families. New York: St. Martin's, 1999.

Breaking the Patterns of Depression. New York: Random House/Doubleday, 1997.

Suggestions of Abuse: True and False Memories of Childhood Sexual Trauma. New York: Simon & Schuster, 1994.

Free Yourself from Depression. Emmaus, PA.: Rodale Press, 1992.

Hypnosis and the Treatment of Depressions: Strategies for Change. New York: Brunner/Mazel, 1992.

Brief Therapy Approaches to Treating Anxiety and Depression (Editor). New York: Brunner/Mazel, 1989.

When Living Hurts: Directives for Treating Depression. New York: Brunner/Mazel, 1988.

Hypnotic and Strategic Interventions: Principles and Practice (Editor). New York: Irvington, 1986.

Taking Hypnosis to the Next Level:

Valuable Tips for Enhancing Your Clinical Practice

Yapko Publications
P.O. Box 487
Fallbrook, CA 92088-0487

For information about permission to reproduce selections from this book, write to Permissions, Yapko Publications,
P.O. Box 487, Fallbrook, CA 92088-0487
E-mail: "Contact Us" form on www.yapko.com

For information about special bulk purchase discounts, please contact Special Sales, Yapko Publications,
P.O. Box 487, Fallbrook, CA. 92088-0487
E-mail: "Contact Us" form on www.yapko.com

ISBN: 978-0-9910796-5-0 (pbk)
ISBN: 978-0-9910796-6-7 (ebk)

Dedication

To my lifelong best friends, Wendy and Richard Horowitz, who have been by my side every step of the way, sharing our lives with a closeness and love that is precious. And, to Megan Horowitz, the daughter we "share," who fills my heart with love and pride.

Acknowledgments

My wife, Diane, is the one who loves, inspires, cajoles, challenges and supports me in more ways than I can count. 41 years of marriage later, there's still no one else with whom I'd rather spend my life.

I am grateful to have the chance to acknowledge that my siblings, Brian, Jerry, Ken, Jackie and Mitchell remain a stabilizing and loving force in my life. Having their support, encouragement and unconditional love through the challenges that life brings to us all is a gift I do not take for granted.

I was lucky enough to know many of the most influential historical figures in the hypnosis field, the pioneers who helped shape the modern practice of clinical hypnosis with their insight and foresight. I especially want to acknowledge Jay Haley, William S. Kroger, and André Weitzenhoffer, for their generous contributions to my professional development.

I am grateful to Jeffrey Zeig, a great friend and colleague for more than 35 years. Jeff has been the driving force in catalyzing a modern and innovative practice of hypnosis through his passionate development and teaching of Milton Erickson's methods.

When I shared with a recent training group my intention to do this book of tips for enhancing practitioners' use of hypnosis, Canadian physician Ron Ireland went to great lengths to put together a list of some of the tips provided in my training he wanted me to consider including in this book. I am thankful he did, because many of those on his list are included here.

Finally, I want to thank all the attendees of my comprehensive clinical hypnosis and strategic psychotherapy programs over the years. Your insights about ways to continually improve and expand the use of hypnosis have been most inspiring.

Table of Contents

A Note to the Reader

Your expectations are the basis for many of your judgments. If the movie or restaurant you go to, or the book you're reading, lives up to your expectations, then you're satisfied. If they don't, then you're disappointed. But, what if your expectations are unrealistic? Unrealistic expectations are too often the basis for disappointment, a preventable consequence when you are clear about what to expect.

So, with that in mind, be aware that this is not a book about "how to do" hypnosis. Rather, this is a book about *how to do hypnosis better*. It is assumed that you already have (or are currently undergoing) formal training in the use of hypnosis. Presumably, you have learned about the nature of hypnosis and hypnotic phenomena, you know how to and already have performed hypnotic inductions with clients, and you already conduct hypnosis sessions in your clinical practice. Thus, there won't be a list of hypnosis techniques to use nor will there be definitions of hypnosis terminology provided here.*

When you have a practical, working knowledge of hypnosis, you inevitably discover that the approaches that work well for one person do not necessarily work as well for another. While no one is 100 percent successful in all their interventions, there are many ways to continually enhance your effectiveness as a clinician. This book provides practical tips for hypnosis practitioners to integrate into their work. They hold the potential to make treatments with hypnosis more deliberate and successful. I hope and expect you'll find them thought provoking and helpful.

MDY

*For the "how to do hypnosis" book that explains concepts, terminology and provides techniques, please see my detailed textbook, *Trancework: An Introduction to the Practice of Clinical Hypnosis,* currently in its fourth edition (with a forthcoming 5th edition in progress as of this writing). It is the text that many hypnosis societies and organizations around the world use because of its comprehensive review of the literature and practical nature. It has been translated into many other languages.

Introduction

Anyone who practices clinical hypnosis does so with the firmly entrenched and therapeutically invaluable belief that people have many more abilities than they consciously realize. Hypnosis engenders an entirely optimistic appraisal of people, thereby giving rise to therapies organized around the belief that people can *discover* and *develop* the specific resources within themselves they will need in order to improve. Hypnosis creates a focused, energized, high-powered context for people to explore, discover, and use more of their innate abilities.

Hypnosis isn't the therapy, and hypnosis itself cures *nothing*. Rather, hypnosis is the *vehicle* for connecting (associating) people to the abilities and realizations that ultimately serve to help them. More to the point, it isn't the experience of hypnosis itself that's therapeutic. Rather, it's what happens *during* hypnosis in terms of developing new and helpful associations that has the potential to be therapeutic.

The study of applied clinical hypnosis, then, revolves around these practical questions:

1. How can we co-create a context that promotes experiential learning?;
2. How can we identify which latent resources may be accessible in a given individual's experience of hypnosis?;
3. How can we structure the development of new therapeutic resources previously unknown and undeveloped in the client?; and,
4. How can we bring these resources forth at the times and places that will best serve the client?

The tips provided herein will speak to these questions and help provide a framework for responding to them with an emphasis on practicality.

Hypnosis is a highly subjective experience. It continues to defy precise definition and objective measurement. Thus, there is plenty of room for wide variations in how professionals conceptualize and practice hypnosis. Debates continue, albeit a little less noisily than in the past, regarding whether there is a state called hypnosis, what factors account for the differences in hypnotic responsiveness across people, how hypnotic suggestions should be structured for maximum impact, whether hypnotic responsiveness can change or is to be considered a fixed trait, and even whether hypnosis enhances therapeutic outcomes. Experienced practitioners no doubt have firm opinions on these subjects and others as well, but the fact that their opinions differ is noteworthy. No one owns the domain of hypnosis and no single view defines it.

The skills needed to be effective in applying hypnosis are many. When one of my colleagues asked Milton Erickson, M.D., the late psychiatrist whose creativity and insights regarding the use of hypnosis literally re-defined the entire field, how long it should take to become proficient in the practice of hypnosis, he replied in this way, paraphrased: "I've been doing hypnosis for more than 50 years. I've authored many books and scores of articles on the subject. I've hypnotized thousands of people… and, I think I'm starting to get the hang of it!" It wasn't a false modesty underlying Dr. Erickson's response. It was a clear acknowledgment that there are as many variations in response as there are people responding, and there can never come a time when you truly know it all. Knowing this is what keeps hypnosis fresh, challenging, illuminating and inspiring for me.

I've been doing hypnosis regularly for more than 40 years. I've had the honor and good fortune of studying with and learning from many of the field's most prominent figures, too many to name individually. I felt their presence as I wrote this book, and I felt profound gratitude for all they taught me and especially for how they encouraged me to continue learning from my clinical experiences with my clients as well as from my personal life experiences. They were the "greatest generation" of pioneers who shaped the clinical field; they also asked the deeper questions that made hypnosis a respectable topic for researchers to investigate.

Over the decades I've had the chance to observe countless hypnosis demonstrations, personally conduct thousands of hypnosis sessions, and train thousands of other professionals in methods of clinical hypnosis. And, I'd say the same thing as Dr. Erickson, only a little differently: I've learned a lot, but there's still so much that I know I don't know.

Despite my not knowing it all, as if anyone could, there is a lot about hypnosis that I *do* know. I wrote this book with the intention of sharing in a succinct, even blunt, manner some of the many key insights about the practice of clinical hypnosis I've acquired over the decades of study and practice. I hope to give practitioners a "running start" in their quest for competence in applying hypnosis, reducing learning by trial and error and avoiding reinventing the hypnosis wheel.

In this book, I strive to blend the science of hypnosis with the art of hypnosis, knowing full well that no matter how scientifically informed one is, which is important for good practice, hypnosis is still largely an art relying on subjective experience and good judgment. It is the art of hypnosis that speaks to what some people might attribute to "intuition." The clinicians who seem to know exactly what to say often attribute their talent to intuition. The clinicians who seem to come up with just the right metaphor at the right time often say the same thing. But, these are "intuitive" *skills* that develop with practice and clinical experience. I hope to help you develop some of these by speaking to both sides of the hypnosis equation – art and science - in this book. I hope the tips and insights I offer here will be valuable to you in whatever way you may practice hypnosis.

Michael D. Yapko, Ph.D.
www.yapko.com

Part 1:

Before the Tips: Thinking Clearly About Hypnosis Comes First

Before the Tips: Thinking Clearly About Hypnosis Comes First

Hypnosis is an exciting and dynamic field that has held my full attention throughout my entire professional life. During this time, hypnosis has made significant contributions to many different domains of study, including: mental health, behavioral medicine, neuroscience, epigenetics, interpersonal neurobiology, cognitive neuroscience, social psychology, education, and affective neuroscience, to name just a few.

Despite the many advances in our understandings of the complexities of hypnosis, there are many aspects of hypnosis that remain poorly defined, difficult to research, and hard to understand. Consequently, there are still many myths and misconceptions that persist as people strive to make sense of experiences that routinely defy logic.

Something as paradoxically simple yet complicated as suggesting a narrowed attention to the idea that your pain or anxiety can diminish or even disappear, and then it actually *does*, is still mystifying in some ways. Thus, in the absence of precise definitions and irrefutable data about hypnotic phenomena, we make educated guesses about what we think is going on with the person in hypnosis.

It's not an all-or-none consideration, however. There are many things we *do* know with a high level of certainty that can be considered integral to the ethical and competent practice of hypnosis. Many of the things we've learned about hypnosis require *all* of us, including me, to change some of what we think and do as new understandings replace older ones. *To hold the same concepts and use the same terminology of hypnosis now as people did many years ago is neither helpful to our clients nor is it helpful in advancing the field.*

Thus, in this first section, I want to provide some *foundational concepts* (FC) with which I believe most current experts in the field would readily agree. Each of these foundational concepts (FC) will provide a basis for appreciating the practical value of the tips to follow.

List of Foundational Concepts

FC #1: How you think about hypnosis and therapy directly determines how you'll apply hypnosis in your clinical practice.

FC #2: Hypnosis cures *nothing*. It's what happens *during* hypnosis – the new internal associations the client forms – that has the *potential* to be therapeutic.

FC #3: The power is not in your words or suggestions; rather, it's in the client's ability to respond meaningfully to them.

FC #4: Suggestion is inevitable in *any* treatment.

FC #5: Hypnosis sessions are goal-oriented.

FC #6: Hypnosis is more than just relaxation.

FC #7: Hypnosis isn't rational. It's experiential and multi-dimensional.

FC #8: Hypnosis is inherently paradoxical in nature.

FC #9: Every hypnosis session has a structure.

FC #10: The word "trance" to characterize hypnotic experience is a dated and somewhat esoteric term that doesn't really represent the experience of hypnosis very well. Use it judiciously.

FC #11: Dissociation is the foundation of hypnosis.

FC #12: A deeper experience of hypnosis isn't necessarily a better or more clinically effective experience of hypnosis.

FC #13: Hypnosis is not innately benign, requiring a healthy caution in its use.

FC #14: Scripts preclude acknowledging the uniqueness of the client. They're made for *everyone*, which means they're not made for *anyone*.

FC #15: Suggestions are typically state-specific, necessitating the use of post-hypnotic suggestions.

FC #16: People differ in their hypnotic abilities.

FC #17: Hypnotic responsiveness is shaped by multiple factors.

FC #18: You cannot accurately predict how a given individual will respond to hypnotic procedures.

FC #19: Before you dismiss someone as "un-hypnotizable," try varying your approach.

FC #20: Words are symbols representing subjective experiences; they are not the actual experiences themselves.

FC #21: You can't use yourself as the reference point for choosing techniques or understanding someone else's experience.

FC #22: There are many reasons why someone may not remember much from his or her childhood. Don't jump to the conclusion it's because of trauma.

FC #23: Not all problems have a specific cause to justify looking for the "reason."

FC #24: You can't teach a client what you don't know.

PART 1

FC #1 How you think about hypnosis and therapy directly determines how you'll apply hypnosis in your clinical practice.

It has been said that there are currently more than 500 distinct models of psychotherapy in use, each with different, often even conflicting, theoretical assumptions, clinical emphases and approaches to treatment. Similarly, there are many different models of hypnosis, each with a different underlying rationale, focal point, and style of practice. When there are so many different models available to choose from when providing clinical services, why choose one approach over another? Clearly, your choice is more a reflection of *your* beliefs and personal preferences than anything else.

When a practitioner learns hypnosis, he or she may learn only a singular approach or may be exposed to a more diverse range of views and practices, depending on the quality of the training received. Through one's training in hypnosis, each practitioner evolves an understanding and style for employing hypnosis that most suits him or her, fitting best to what he or she is comfortable doing and believes works best. This process of filtering information and making judgments based on one's preferences is inevitable, of course, and it highlights the primary reason why different people think about and practice hypnosis so differently. **When there are so many different ways to think about and apply hypnosis, it's important to appreciate that it is less about being *right*, ("my way is the right way") and more about being *effective*.** There are lots of "right" ways to do hypnosis, meaning there are diverse ways of applying hypnosis that can produce good therapeutic results. The true skill lies in choosing an approach the client will respond to rather than simply employing an approach you just happen to like.

FC #2 Hypnosis cures *nothing*. It's what happens *during* hypnosis – the new internal associations the client forms - that has the *potential* to be therapeutic.

People routinely ask the question, "Can hypnosis help with my problem?" People mistakenly believe that hypnosis is the active ingredient in treatment. However, hypnosis in and of itself doesn't provide the cure for *any* problem. Rather, hypnosis provides a context, a vehicle, for introducing ideas, information, experiences and perspectives that have the *potential* to alter the way someone feels, thinks or reacts.

The mere fact that the person is focused or absorbed in the experience of hypnosis does not mean he or she will necessarily respond to or integrate anything the clinician has to say. The clinician provides opportunities for the client to absorb something meaningful by employing carefully worded suggestions that have the *potential* to be helpful. The new understandings, the new associations or links the client forms while attending to the clinician's suggestions, represent the potential benefits of treatment during hypnosis.

No matter how deeply hypnotized someone might be, if the suggestions aren't relevant and meaningful to the client, they will have little or no therapeutic effect.

FC #3 The power is not in your words or suggestions; rather, it's in the client's ability to respond meaningfully to them.

Though we a may share a common language with someone, using the same words and syntax, how each person interprets and relates to a word or phrase is entirely idiosyncratic. Words represent experiences and are not the experience themselves. For example, we can talk about "hypnosis" and how valuable a therapeutic tool it is. But, only further analysis will reveal whether we share the same definition and understanding of the experience of hypnosis or how to best use it therapeutically. So, if we only use the same term, hypnosis, without greater clarification about our perspectives, we could easily think we mean the same thing.

Each person's experience is necessarily and inevitably different from the experience of others. Thus, when using language as the means of conveying ideas or as the stimulus for some experience in hypnosis, it helps to be aware that whatever words you use will be interpreted and responded to by the client with unique associations that you may not be able to fully predict.

This is especially true the more abstract your language. Abstract or poorly defined terms invite greater projection of meaning. Since shared words don't necessarily make for a shared meaning, it's desirable to be observant as to any unusual reactions. Checking in with the client during the process as to how he or she is responding and debriefing the client afterwards about his or her experience will help to minimize misinterpretations. These are good ways to bridge the inevitable gap, small or large, between the intentions of your suggestions and the effects they actually generate. The quality of the suggestions you offer is important, of course, but how your client relates to them is even more important.

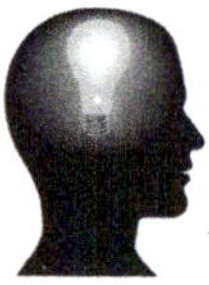

FC #4 Suggestion is inevitable in *any* treatment.

Hypnosis is fascinating for a great many reasons, but one insight that makes it especially worthy of study relates to its in-depth consideration of the *potential* power of suggestion. Suggestion is not unique to hypnosis, though. In fact, suggestion is innate to *any* form of treatment, inextricably tied to the way a treatment is conceived and delivered.

The typical medical suggestions, "Take these pills and you'll feel better" or "Have this procedure and you'll make a full recovery" are obvious in what they suggest. Likewise, the typical psychotherapeutic suggestions, "You'll feel better when you talk about what's bothering you" or, "Doing this exercise will be helpful to you" are equally obvious. Less obvious, though, is how suggestion can be implied rather than directly stated, making the role of suggestion in the treatment process easier to miss.

Realistically, you can't even ask a question without suggesting something. If I ask you, "So, how do you *feel* about that?", I'm suggesting you turn your attention inwardly and make an emotional appraisal you can then share with me verbally. If I ask, "So, what do you *think* about that?", I'm suggesting you focus internally to a different aspect of your experience, namely your cognitions or thoughts, and again make an appraisal you can share with me verbally. I'm asking routine questions, but they contain suggestions for taking specific actions on your part. Suggestion can't be completely avoided, nor does it need to be. It's an inevitable part of interaction in general, and therapeutic interaction in particular. Since you can't escape being suggestive, the goal is to employ suggestions skillfully.

FC #5 Hypnosis sessions are goal-oriented.

Whenever you conduct a clinical hypnosis session, there is a goal in mind, a reason you're using hypnosis to create the possibility of some therapeutic result. A critically important starting point for any hypnosis session is having a clear idea about its objectives. When a goal is either absent or poorly defined, it is too easy for the session to be aimless and unproductive. That's an undesirable outcome for a variety of reasons, not the least of which is it can stall or even prevent positive outcomes later. After all, when a client endures a session that went nowhere, he or she can easily feel discouraged, frustrated, even angry, and develop a negative expectation for further treatment that leads to poor treatment results or the client dropping out of therapy altogether. It can also lead to the erroneous conclusion that "hypnosis doesn't work" when, in fact, it was a poorly defined or executed session that simply did not meet that particular client's needs.

So, there is a definite pressure to make each session count, moving the client forward, if even slightly, to build and keep some momentum going in the therapy. My advice is straightforward: If you can't define the session's goals in 25 words or less, then don't do the session. It will simply be too unfocused. "Going fishing" by doing hypnosis and simply hoping that *something* useful happens isn't always a bad thing, but it may prove costly to the client if the fishing expedition yields nothing substantive. Having a goal in mind and ways to structure the session to reach that goal are keys to an effective practice of hypnosis.

FC #6 Hypnosis is more than just relaxation.

Helping people relax can be a good therapeutic intervention, particularly when stress-related problems are predominant. Relaxation provides them with a direct experience that highlights the message, "Your subjective experience is malleable." This is an important message when talking to someone about the possibilities of change.

Helping people relax can help reduce fear and hypervigilance. It can build greater receptivity to new ideas and help the client acquire new information, perspective and skills more easily. Relaxation feels good, providing an experience of comfort people often miss in their highly stressed and fast paced lives. Furthermore, for better or worse, clients often gauge the value or success of their hypnotic experience according to how relaxed they felt during the session.

But, as valuable as relaxation can be, hypnosis is more than just relaxing. What matters even more is how engaged the person is in the experience, how absorbed he or she is in the things you talk about during the course of the session, and how able he or she is to actually integrate and use your suggestions. If the person is relaxed, but your suggestions don't fit well, then the relaxation alone will not generate a meaningful therapeutic result.

Can someone be in hypnosis but not be relaxed? Yes, most certainly. "Active-alert" forms of hypnosis are typically employed when peak performance (such as in an athletic competition or test performance) precludes having one's eyes closed and relaxing. Relaxation provides a nice foundation for the hypnotic interaction, but a good hypnosis session can involve so much more than just providing a relaxing experience.

There are times in therapy when the goal isn't to provide comfort. An advanced hypnotic technique, such as the "confusion technique," can be great for building absorption, but it is innately uncomfortable since people don't generally like to be confused. Furthermore, sometimes the client is *too* comfortable with something he or she *shouldn't* be, such as drinking too much or tolerating an abusive relationship. As clinicians, we definitely want to *comfort the afflicted...* but it is also true that sometimes we may need to *afflict* the comfortable.

Awh

FC #7 Hypnosis isn't rational. It's experiential and multi-dimensional.

Human beings may be capable of rationality in some arenas but, in general, we aren't rational creatures. While learning to think and behave more logically would be of great help in many circumstances, there are many other circumstances where logic is irrelevant. Falling in love, being moved by a song, fantasizing about winning the lottery, and countless other such experiences aren't based on logic. When someone's irrational feelings are the foundation of their thoughts, reactions, choices, behavior, and connections to others, how can we best connect them to other aspects of experience that can yield better outcomes? Sometimes that might mean connecting them to a more rational, objective perspective, while other times it might mean using non-rational suggestions to make a meaningful point.

Hypnosis is an approach that emphasizes the power of subjective experience to shape perceptions and choices. Hypnosis often encourages responses that are seemingly illogical. Many of the suggestions given during hypnosis make little sense on a rational level yet give rise to often dramatic therapeutic responses. This is one of the things, among many, that make hypnosis so inherently fascinating. People can respond to suggestions that do not make sense ("You can go roller blading on the rings of Saturn") with experiential responses that make *perfect* sense ("I feel so free!").

These non-logical but meaningful responses can exist on many different levels of experience. For example, on the physiological level, suggesting to someone that he or she can experience a numb hand that can transfer the numbness to another part of the body experiencing pain and thereby reduce or eliminate the pain there (a technique known as a "glove anesthesia") isn't logical. But, it can generate amazing consequences in terms of pain relief. Other levels include *cognitive* responses such as new thoughts or insights, *emotional* responses such as relief or a newly found courage, *behavioral* responses such as taking

PART I

a new course of action, and/or *spiritual* responses when the person is moved by an emergent new meaning or self-awareness. Hypnosis can serve as a catalyst for a deeper and richer quality of life.

You have to expand the little things through out you day that you can control, Your energy Moving you down progress lane. Change is a detour & you get to direct it.

FC #8 Hypnosis is inherently paradoxical in nature.

Hypnosis involves paradox, messages that seem to be mutually contradictory. One of the many interesting things about hypnosis is how people in hypnosis process information differently than when they're not in hypnosis. This is true for how they process sensory input, memory, autobiographical memory, as well as incongruent and even paradoxical messages. The paradoxical nature of messages in hypnosis is especially evident when hypnosis is applied in clinical practice.

PART 1

Consider these examples:

- Part of what makes hypnosis "special" is that it *isn't* special - after all, hypnosis occurs routinely in daily life whenever we get absorbed (such as in the common example of so-called "highway hypnosis");
- Hypnosis encourages a deep connection to your internal experience, yet you're partly or fully detached from the usual cues you might normally respond to;
- You're given suggestions for how to respond, but encouraged to respond spontaneously;
- You're told stories (metaphors) about other people so the story clearly isn't about you, but the story really *is* about you, which is why you're being told the story;
- You're given suggestions that might be confusing as a means of encouraging clarity;
- You're acknowledged as unique… just like everyone else; and,
- You're encouraged to make something happen by being told not to try to make anything happen.

The paradoxes embedded in hypnosis represent an opportunity to go beyond logic *or* rationality in order to learn experientially. The path you follow during a hypnosis session - as either the clinician or client - isn't necessarily a straightforward one when paradox is innate to the process. But, seemingly paradoxically perhaps, the path can still be the most expedient way to get people where they want to go.

FC #9 Every hypnosis session has a structure.

Hypnosis sessions inevitably have an innate structure within them, components that can be identified regardless of what the style or content of the session might be. Every hypnosis session has a beginning, middle, and end. But, we can be much more specific as to what the general or generic structure of a session will be.

Any session will first involve an *orientation to hypnosis*, a point where any discussion about hypnosis and its potential value in the client's therapy turns to initiating the hypnotic interaction. Then, the *hypnotic induction* begins, using whatever method or approach the clinician employs to begin to focus and direct the client's attention. The clinician then strives to *build a response set*, establishing a momentum of enhanced responsiveness on the part of the client such that responsiveness increases over the course of the session. Next, the clinician begins to *address the therapeutic goals* of the session, whether through direct or indirect suggestions, introducing shifts in perceptions on whatever levels deemed therapeutically important. The clinician may or may not interact with the client during hypnosis based on his or her style and methodology. The clinician will then provide some form of *post-hypnotic suggestions* to facilitate an integration of the new ideas and experiences from the session into the salient portions of the client's life, called "contextualization." The clinician then provides suggestions for *attaining a closure* to the session and then, as the final step in the sequence, *disengaging or fully re-orienting* from hypnosis.

How someone conducts a session can vary dramatically from one practitioner to another based on many factors (such as theoretical orientation and personal style), but no matter who is doing hypnosis in whatever way they may do it, there will always be these universal structural components evident in their work.

PART 1

FC #10 The word "trance" to characterize hypnotic experience is a dated and somewhat esoteric term that doesn't really represent the experience of hypnosis very well. Use it judiciously.

The word "trance" is one of the most archaic ways of describing the experience of hypnosis. Like so many other terms that are tied to the early days of hypnosis, it's time to update the vocabulary. The word "trance" suggests some unusual state of consciousness, something markedly different from your usual qualities of awareness.

Being in hypnosis is a difference of degree, not kind, in the degree of focus and connection to the usual environmental cues. Being "put into a trance state" doesn't really speak to what's happening and implies something quite different than what actually occurs. Research on this subject shows that when people were asked, "Were you in a trance?" at the end of a hypnosis session, the great majority of people replied, "No, I wasn't." Apparently, they had some preconceptions about what it means to be in a trance, and whatever experience they had with hypnosis didn't meet those criteria.

Reporting you have been focused, absorbed, deeply engaged, or highly attentive, are far more meaningful ways of describing the experience of being in hypnosis than saying you were in a trance. The modern neuroscientists who study the phenomenon of hypnosis virtually never use the word trance. Instead they define their domain of study as "attention." This is a much more realistic framing of what we're considering when we conduct hypnosis: How does the person's attention get focused, and then how might that focused attention give rise to the various hypnotic phenomena that are used therapeutically?

I describe hypnosis as "attention with intention." You might prefer another way of describing it, but whatever way you choose to represent hypnosis, the more closely it fits a client's actual experience, the better. Calling it a "trance state" isn't really wrong. It's just that it's not right, either.

I'd like to briefly address what may seem like an obvious contradiction regarding titling my hypnosis textbook *Trancework* given what I've just said about using the word "trance." When I titled the first edition in 1984, I obviously still used the word trance. But, times change, and I would now choose a different title if I had it to do over again. Since the book has well over 30 years of history and a strong reputation, to change the title now as it approaches its forthcoming fifth edition would be confusing.

FC #11 Dissociation is the foundation of hypnosis.

While relaxation is often a component of hypnosis procedures, it is *not* an essential component of hypnosis. However, without dissociation present to one degree or another, hypnosis does not occur.

Dissociation is defined as the breaking down of global experiences into their component parts. Dissociation involves a *separation* of subjective elements of experience. These may be: *cognitive* elements (as in separating executive functioning from orienting or alerting attentional subsystems), *physical* elements (as in separating the painful limb from the rest of the body), *temporal* elements (as in separating the painful past from the hopeful future), or *emotional* elements (as in separating feelings from choice of action), to name just a few examples.

Dissociation allows for the *automaticity* of hypnotic responses, the involuntary or non-volitional nature of people generating hypnotic phenomena such as age regression or sensory alterations without any sense of intentional effort. Structurally, every clinical hypnosis session is going to involve elements of *dissociation*, moving people *away from* some aspects of their experience, and its counterpart *association*, moving people *closer* to other aspects of their experience.

What specific aspects of subjective experience a clinician will want to move someone closer to ("get in touch with your feelings") or further away from ("get *out* of touch with your feelings") depends entirely on the therapeutic goals and the clinician's therapeutic style. But, as soon as you begin the induction of hypnosis, you have begun to facilitate dissociation, the primary goal of performing an induction.

Helping the client to experience an amplification of some experiences while encouraging others to recede into the background is inevitable as soon as the client's field of attention begins to narrow. The more absorbed the person becomes in the hypnotic experience, the more *detached* he or she becomes from usual environmental and even internal cues. The more independently different aspects of experience become that normally operate synergistically, the greater the degree of dissociation.

FC #12 A deeper experience of hypnosis isn't necessarily a better or more clinically effective experience of hypnosis.

The mere fact that someone is in hypnosis doesn't assure you that your suggestions are more likely to be accepted and integrated by the client. As stated earlier, hypnosis itself isn't curative or therapeutic; rather, it's what happens *during* hypnosis that has those potentials.

When hypnosis was thought to be a "special state" that made people in hypnosis more receptive to suggestions, a misinformed view that still underlies many peoples' misconceptions about hypnosis, many believed that you'd get a higher level of compliance from the client the more deeply into hypnosis they went. It was further assumed in those early days of hypnosis that the goal was to get the client "deeper and deeper" into hypnosis in order to elicit more complex hypnotic phenomena (such as anesthesia). Thus, early conceptualizations of the relationship between the ability to produce hypnotic phenomena and the "depth" of hypnosis established a "trance level-hypnotic response" paradigm.

The assumption was that in a "light trance" the hypnotized client would only generate easier or milder manifestations of hypnosis, and that those in "medium level trances" would be able to generate more complex hypnotic phenomena, and those in a "deep trance" and the even deeper "somnambule" level would be able to generate the most complex hypnotic phenomena. But, this "trance level A catalyzes hypnotic response B " is untrue.

The research has been unambiguous about the fact that people in "lighter" hypnotic experiences are quite capable of generating complex responses that were previously presumed to only be possible during "deeper" experiences. Likewise, there are many people who have "deeper" hypnotic experiences yet can't generate presumably simpler responses.

The incantations so many practitioners use to get a client to "go deeper and deeper" aren't nearly as important to therapeutic success as was previously believed. It became evident that the depth of hypnosis wasn't the determining factor as to what someone was capable of generating in terms of hypnotic – or therapeutic – responses. Simply put, a deeper experience of hypnosis isn't necessarily a better or more productive one.

PART 1

FC #13 Hypnosis is not innately benign, requiring a healthy caution in its use.

Hypnosis is a tool, and, like any tool, it can easily be misapplied. It is a basic truth that anything that has the potential to help also has the potential to harm, whether it's a drug, a piece of advice, a surgical procedure or any other form of treatment. Thus, a well-intentioned suggestion can end up having unexpected negative consequences simply because of the gap between the clinician's intended meaning and the way the client interpreted and reacted to what was either said or merely *implied.*

When a treatment leads someone to get worse, not better, it is called *iatrogenic.* Iatrogenesis is not at all unique to hypnosis and, in fact, occurs in every arena of treatment medically or psychologically. The goal, of course, is to prevent iatrogenic responses by being a well-informed, perceptive clinician and avoiding the pitfalls as best as one can.

Some of the greatest dangers associated with poor practice include:

- The clinician being poorly trained in hypnosis and, unwittingly, relying on outdated misinformation and methods which can delay or even prevent positive results, misinformation which he or she then also passes on to the client as fact;

- Mismanaging the strong emotional reactions that can arise in the client during the course of treatment;

- Inadvertently reinforcing the client's patterns that gave rise to their symptoms;

- Providing suggestions that are based on personal beliefs or assumptions that are not shared by or acceptable to the client;

- Demanding or even just expecting the client to respond "correctly" to your suggestions and mishandling the interaction when he or she doesn't do so;

- Reinforcing "magical thinking" and unrealistic expectations on the part of the client;

- Unintended suggestions for developing negative experiences (the "nocebo effect"); and,

- Implanting false memories intentionally or unintentionally or otherwise encouraging the adoption of convenient but inaccurate beliefs about the reasons for one's problems.

Recognizing that hypnosis can cause unintentional harm is the basis for being well-trained and only using hypnosis within the scope of one's clinical expertise. To be clear, it's not the hypnosis itself that is dangerous, rather it's the way it can be misapplied.

FC #14 Scripts preclude acknowledging the uniqueness of the client. They're made for *everyone*, which means they're not made for *anyone*.

Many people practice hypnosis by using prepared scripts published in articles or books. These scripts literally provide a word-for-word "canned" approach to the use of hypnosis, as if these "magic words" delivered as written are going to assure therapeutic success.

There are scripts readily available for every problem you can think of, and these scripts are often read verbatim to the client by those clinicians who practice hypnosis in this way. Some scripts are quite creative and multi-dimensional, while others are poorly conceived and structured. Regardless of how good the script might be, though, it is still a script. It inevitably speaks to clients in an impersonal way since the script was not created for that specific individual.

Thus, 10 clients may come in to, say, stop smoking, and even though each person is quite different from the others in countless ways, they all hear the same script simply because they happen to share the bad habit of smoking. There is no ability to acknowledge the uniqueness of someone if you simply run him or her through a "cookie cutter" approach. Scripts may make it easier on the clinician not to have to think through the dynamics of a particular client's problems and just respond to the symptom or diagnostic label, and they may make it easier on the clinician to not have to generate anything novel or specific to the client, but what's easier for the clinician isn't usually what's *best* for the client.

A driving force of performing good hypnosis sessions is recognizing the client's strengths, personal resources and unique attributes and incorporating them into the hypnosis session, empowering the person in the process. Scripted approaches can only speak in generalities that may or may not apply to a given individual. It's too much like saying, in essence, "Here's a size 9 shoe, now fit your foot to it."

Scripted approaches will work for some people, of course, which is why they persist. But, to employ an approach that knowingly and deliberately misses the opportunity to speak to the unique attributes of your client is simply a shame. Furthermore, when the script doesn't have the desired effect, the clinician can too easily think the client is resistant and the client can too easily conclude, "hypnosis doesn't work." Good hypnosis training teaches you to tailor your approach to better fit the individual client's needs and makeup, thereby increasing the likelihood of the intervention succeeding.

FC #15 Suggestions are typically state-specific, necessitating the use of post-hypnotic suggestions.

The term "state-specificity" refers to a subjective experience that is tied to a particular state, an association within the individual tied to both internal and external (contextual) cues. This is the essence of what clinical hypnosis is about: clinicians strive to help the client manage some previously troublesome situation (or thought or feeling) by engaging in a more effective response that was developed during the hypnosis session.

When someone is in hypnosis, he or she is capable of generating a wide range of condensed and non-volitional experiences, such as age regression or analgesia. The clinician helps develop and use the hypnotically generated experience toward some therapeutic objective, and the experience can be quite powerful for the client. But, this experience was generated during hypnosis and, through state-specificity, is tied to the experience of hypnosis. The client is most unlikely to continue to experience the regression or analgesia once the hypnosis session is ended *unless* suggestions are given or the client chooses to do so.

The lack of a spontaneous carryover from the hypnosis session into the client's life was the basis for the common criticism hypnosis faced early on that it only generated temporary results and thus wasn't all that valuable a tool in treatment. It was, at least in part, a valid criticism. What wasn't known then that is known now is the "state-specific" nature of hypnotic responses, necessitating the use of a vehicle for deliberately extending the experiences and relevant learnings from the hypnosis session into the areas of the client's life where they would be beneficial. The vehicle for accomplishing this is the "post-hypnotic suggestion." The post-hypnotic suggestion is a suggestion given to the client during hypnosis to associate the achievements made during hypnosis to relevant contexts of the client's life. The post-hypnotic suggestion is essential to extending the benefits of hypnosis beyond just the hypnosis session itself.

FC #16 People differ in their hypnotic abilities.

There aren't very many things about hypnosis that all experts agree upon, but this is one of those rare points of agreement: People vary widely in their ability to respond meaningfully to hypnosis. Why that is and what it means about individual differences is the subject of serious scientific debate, with reasonable hypotheses asserted by a wide array of experts that may challenge and even contradict each other. Even the terminology associated with this issue is open for discussion. Are we talking about hypnotizability? Hypnotic susceptibility? Hypnotic responsiveness? Hypnotic talent? Capacity for absorption? Attentional style? How do we define, describe and measure the differences between individuals' responses to hypnosis?

Bypassing, at least for the moment, these complex issues, the salient point of this section is recognizing that how you think about what factors account for these differences will significantly influence your style of practice. For example, if you think of hypnosis as a biological phenomenon, one that may even be genetically based as some studies have suggested, then when you encounter someone who doesn't respond well to your approach, it may be easy to conclude he or she is "lacking the hypnosis gene." As a result, you might be unwilling to do hypnosis with someone deemed incapable of hypnosis. Or, conversely, if you believe that everyone is capable of responding to hypnosis, when you encounter someone who doesn't, you might try to analyze his or her "resistance." Some even go so far as to assert that the lack of responsiveness is a form of pathology rooted in the client's "need" for his or her symptoms.

I think the most practical position to take regarding the differences across individuals is one of "therapeutic curiosity." You cannot predict with any certainty whether or how someone will respond to your hypnotic methods. So, as you move from the interview to the induction of hypnosis phase, you can be curious about the client's hypnotic abilities and how you might help him or her connect to those abilities. This is a way to positively reinforce the development and use of whatever natural hypnotic talents he or she might have to whatever degree he or she has them.

FC #17 Hypnotic responsiveness is shaped by multiple factors.

My personal preference is the term "hypnotic responsiveness" when addressing the general topic of peoples' quality of experience in hypnosis. Hypnotic responsiveness in a given individual at a particular moment is shaped by many different factors.

Some of these are *personal factors,* such as: the person's past experience with or type of exposure to hypnosis, comfort with hypnotic procedures and the subjective alterations that accompany them, mood, expectations about what will or should happen in hypnosis, fears that may arise from misconceptions about hypnosis, and any impairments to the ability to focus attention because of intrusive or distressing symptoms.

Other factors are *interpersonal,* such as: the level of trust for the clinician, the appropriateness of hypnosis to the type of relationship that has been agreed upon, the quality of communication between clinician and client that encompasses informed consent and acceptable rationales for including hypnosis in treatment, and an affirmation that makes it clear the client can respond to whatever degree he or she wishes based on the appropriateness and relevance of the provided suggestions.

The third domain of factors influencing hypnotic responsiveness are *contextual,* such as: the physical environment and whether its characteristics support or challenge the ability to focus, the nature of the context and whether it is defined as educational, clinical, experimental, or something else. These are just some of the many factors that influence peoples' ability to respond meaningfully to hypnosis, highlighting the complexities of effective hypnotic interaction and provides yet another reason why a "one size fits all" approach is unlikely to succeed.

FC #18 You cannot accurately predict how a given individual will respond to hypnotic procedures.

There are many different formal tests that have been developed over the years that attempt to define and measure the characteristic of hypnotic responsiveness. A great deal of research has gone into developing the normative data on these tests (validity and reliability) across many different research populations. Despite the great efforts many have made to develop a test that meets the challenge of pre-determining someone's hypnotic abilities, there is no specific test or measure that has proven to be fully up to the task.

If you administer a formal test, are you measuring someone's hypnotic ability, or are you measuring someone's response to the test items? Will the responses to the impersonal test items predict responses to personal therapeutic suggestions? The motivations and abilities drawn upon when giving impersonal suggestions as part of a test protocol may have little bearing on how someone will respond when responding to suggestions that are well tailored, personally meaningful, and which address important clinical issues.

Furthermore, how someone responds to some suggestions doesn't predict how that same person will respond to other suggestions. Hypnotic responsiveness isn't a fixed trait that indicates a uniform quality of responding across different types of suggestions. Someone may do very well with suggestions for, say, age regression, but not do very well when given suggestions for sensory alterations. If you want to know how someone is going to respond to hypnosis, then do hypnosis with him or her.

PART 1

FC #19 Before you dismiss someone as "un-hypnotizable," try varying your approach.

While it is beyond question that people differ in their hypnotic abilities, what is far less clear is *why* they differ and what that might mean for applying clinical hypnosis in practice. Research on large groups of people exposed to standardized approaches to hypnosis, as in the use of formal test protocols, have yielded statistics that suggest a certain percentage of people are highly hypnotizable, a certain percentage of people are either minimal or non-responders, and the majority of people are somewhere in-between.

If you perform an induction on someone who responds minimally or not at all, should you conclude that this individual is a so-called "low hypnotizable?" And, does that mean, then, that hypnosis isn't going to be helpful and therefore shouldn't be used? It's tempting to jump to this easy conclusion, but it isn't necessarily the right conclusion to reach. If you view the capacity for hypnosis as innate to the client, believing they either have hypnotic ability to one degree or another or they don't, then it is easier to employ scripted or direct approaches and dismiss the client as un-hypnotizable if he or she doesn't respond well to those methods. But, if you view hypnosis as at least partly a product of an interaction, then will a more personalized approach increase the likelihood of a better response? This issue has often been debated and the positions people take are, as you might predict, mixed.

Some practitioners are convinced that hypnosis is a fixed trait that does not change over time. Others believe hypnosis varies with motivation, context, experience, and so forth, and since it varies responsiveness can increase with practice and the use of varied approaches. I am in this latter group, convinced that someone's hypnotic abilities can be enhanced with varied and well-tailored approaches.

If you try an approach and it doesn't go as well as you and the client would like, try another approach that is different enough from the first one that may make a helpful difference. It's invaluable to have a mix of approaches that vary from each other in structure and style in your repertoire. Then you can try different ones and see which of them your client can respond to most beneficially.

FC #20 Words are symbols representing subjective experiences; they are not the actual experiences themselves.

How people process language is immediately relevant to the qualities of experience they generate in general, and especially during hypnosis. The language you use as a clinician in conducting hypnosis sessions is intended to produce specific responses. Which words should you use? Whatever words you say, the client will, of course, have to link them to some internal experience associated with that word. This is how we make meaning. If I say the word "elephant," in order to understand what I've said, you have to attach that word to some inner representation of an elephant. The word is merely a symbol that represents the reality of an elephant. What your inner representation is, I cannot know until you share it with me. Will it be an image of an elephant? A memory of a story you saw on TV involving elephants? A memory of being on safari in Africa and seeing elephants in the wild? As discussed previously, your associations will be uniquely yours, such that even when we use the same words it doesn't mean we share the same meaning.

Words are triggers for experiences, and whatever words you say to your client will carry a variety of associations with them, including cognitive, emotional, sensory, and physical associations. Thus, word choice matters. Some of the compelling reasons to be especially cognizant of your word choices come from neuroscientific studies of the effects of different kinds of language on subjective experience. Neuroimaging studies suggest that the same regions of the brain that are involved with actual sensory experience or performing actions are also involved in representing concepts. On a sensory level, using words that represent sensory experiences such as specific smells (such as lavender or cinnamon) elicit responses from the language processing parts of our brains but also from those areas that process smells. When researchers using brain scanners asked participants to read words with strong odor associations, those words "lit up" the primary olfactory cortex whereas neutral words did not. Similarly, when words that involved texture were used (such as leathery or velvety), the sensory cortex activated but did not become active when only neutral words were used.

The neuroscientific evidence supports observations made long ago in the hypnosis literature that the more emotional and sensory based your use of language, the fuller a response you are likely to get from the client. He or she is processing those suggestions on multiple levels of experience.

FC #21 You can't use yourself as the reference point for choosing techniques or understanding someone else's experience.

A commonly held view of hypnosis is reflected in statements such as, "I tried hypnosis. It didn't work for me, so I don't believe in hypnosis" and, "I'm skeptical about hypnosis because I don't think anyone can really do those things they claim. I know *I can't*."

Understandably, people form a global or over-general view of hypnosis based on their personal experience. While that may be understandable, it is a mistake to do so. To assume that your own experience with something, almost *anything* for that matter, represents the entire category of that phenomenon and even predicts how others will react, is a self-centered, egocentric position to take. In a broader perspective, you come to understand that other people can do things and experience things that, for whatever reason, you cannot. (Likewise, you can do and experience things that others cannot.) As an example, although I am quite responsive to good hypnotic procedures, I can't produce a full hypnotic anesthesia in a part of my body in just a few seconds the way some "hypnotic virtuosos" can. I require more time than that, but eventually I'll get there. Am I then justified in saying, "If I can't do it, then *nobody* can and people who say they do are faking?" Of course not.

There are people who can indeed quickly and reliably demonstrate hypnotic abilities that other people cannot. This is the basis for my earlier point that the best mindset a good clinician has as he or she does hypnosis is a healthy curiosity about what some individual's hypnotic talents are.

As I begin my sessions with people, I have no idea what they can do and am very curious to find out. And, I am routinely amazed when people are able to generate responses that can serve them well, especially when they're responses that I personally can't produce. I'm not the reference point for what others can do... and neither are you.

FC #22 There are many reasons why someone may not remember much from his or her childhood. Don't jump to the conclusion it's because of trauma.

The so-called "memory wars" of the 1990s saw the field deeply divided by those who believed that people would repress memories of childhood abuse that would then surface years later as pervasive and distressing symptoms. Others were more than a little skeptical about repressed memories, wondering what mental mechanism could possibly account for forgetting some of the most emotionally charged experiences one can have.

Serious questions arose: From what age is repression possible? How can one forget dozens or even hundreds of such terrible episodes spanning years? Are they somehow repressed one at a time as they occur or all at once years later? Ultimately, it became clear that the concept of repressed memories worked far better in theory than in real life. The danger, as described in detail in my groundbreaking book, *Suggestions of Abuse* (Simon & Schuster, 1994), is when the clinician infers a history of abuse then strives to "uncover" the memories. Clinicians did not understand that memory is highly responsive to suggestive influences and that *the very act of digging for presumably repressed memories can unintentionally create them.*

Can therapists really lead someone to believe he or she was abused when, in fact, he or she was not? Yes! If not because of trauma, then what other reasons are there as to why someone might remember so little from childhood?

There are many possible reasons, including:

- *Normal childhood amnesia,* the lack of sufficient neurological development to form and retain childhood memories;

- Perceptual *filtering* that precludes noticing stimuli in the first place, thus can't enter long-term storage;

- *Interference,* such as when earlier memories disrupt later ones (proactive) or when later memories disrupt earlier ones (retroactive);

- *Retrieval failure* because the memory has decayed over time and the person unintentionally fills in the blanks with either imagined or suggested details ("confabulation"); and,

- *Neurological problems* affecting normal brain functions.

Clinicians would be wise to study the workings of memory in depth before even considering the possibility of using hypnosis to do any kind of memory work with a client.It is potentially hazardous.

FC #23 Not all problems have a specific cause to justify looking for the "reason."

One of the important distinctions to make in the area of assessment is to distinguish between *event-driven* and *process-driven* problems. Historically, the foundational premise of the psychotherapy field has been that wherever you observe symptoms, there must be some associated causal event that would account for them. This is known as the "linear causation model of symptom etiology." When someone subscribes to this perspective, which generations of psychotherapists did, it is reflexive to assume there is some underlying causal event that gave rise to the clients' symptoms. Thus, this is an "event-driven" perspective.

However, as our understandings of peoples' problems have become more sophisticated and multi-dimensional, the evidence has grown that some of the most common problems people face are generated and maintained by ongoing cognitive and perceptual processes rather than specific events. This is especially (but not always) the case in two of the most common disorders clinicians are asked to treat: anxiety and depression. For example, when someone has a fear of flying, it's obviously not because he or she was in a fatal plane crash. Rather, it's largely because of a perceptual process of being unable to distinguish between an imagined and immediate threat and thus reacting to an imagined threat as if it was a real one. Focusing on detailed mental imagery of being in a doomed plane is enough to generate panic in *anyone*.

If someone is overly dedicated to the event-driven perspective, he or she can still assume there must be some event that made the person highly reactive to airplanes, but this is really a stretch to make the symptoms fit the theory. Those therapeutic interventions that emphasize changing the style of thinking or correcting the errors in thinking, such as cognitive-behavioral therapy (CBT) or rational emotional behavioral therapy (REBT), are successful for this reason. They focus on introducing shifts, in or out of hypnosis, in how the person thinks about or interprets life events that give rise to the symptoms.

Event-driven and process-driven approaches both work quite well. This discussion simply encourages an awareness that one can't just simply assume there's some event in the person's history to uncover and then spend inordinate amounts of therapy time looking for it. It may not be there. Furthermore, you can't really move forward just looking backwards. Regression processes have their place in therapy but, in general, there's far more therapeutic value in building a good future than in rehashing the past.

FC #24 You can't teach a client what you don't know.

By the time someone seeks professional help, with or without hypnosis, he or she has usually been suffering with problems and symptoms for an extended period of time. Furthermore, he or she has likely taken steps meant to resolve the problem but failed in the endeavor. When clients report feeling "stuck" in some area of their life, perhaps feeling helpless and hopeless, they typically don't know what to do to get "unstuck." If you were to ask the client, "If you were going to resolve this issue, what would be your first step?", then you need not be surprised when the client says, "I have no idea." Occasionally a client knows what the next step is and just doesn't like it, but most of the time the client simply doesn't know what to do in order to begin resolving his or her problem.

The tasks of a good clinician, in my opinion, are to provide a viable structure for solving the current problem(s), and a viable structure for effective problem solving in the future. By "viable structure," I mean a series of specific steps the client can follow that will be an effective means of reaching his or her goal(s). This translates into teaching specific skills such as knowing how to define realistic goals, or manage frustration when some desired result isn't immediately forthcoming, or make better decisions. This would require a clinician to have the skills of knowing *how* to teach effective goal setting, frustration tolerance and decision-making. These are routine areas of concern in treatment and they each require a clinician to provide concrete step-by-step strategies for managing them well.

For example, if you are going to teach someone how to better handle frustration and stay on course in some endeavor, a resource called "frustration tolerance," *how* would you do that? Similarly, if you're going to teach other valuable resources such as impulse control, empathy, stress management, and self-acceptance, how would you do so? You may know what these resources are in the abstract, but do you know how to teach them to a client who desperately needs to learn them? It is a challenge every clinician has to rise to – how to make useful and empowering resources more accessible to the client whenever and wherever they are needed. A key limitation is when the clinician doesn't have a well-defined means for doing so. After all, you really *can't* teach what you don't know.

Part 2:

Tips for Establishing a Therapeutic Framework

Tips for Establishing a Therapeutic Framework

Before you begin your hypnosis session, it's important to build a meaningful framework for highlighting the therapeutic merits of using hypnosis. When you present treatment options to your client, or when you respond to direct requests for hypnosis in particular, the way you structure the interaction will either add to or take away from the quality of the client's hypnosis experience. This section provides tips for setting the stage for conducting effective hypnosis sessions.

List of Tips for Establishing a Therapeutic Framework

Tip #1: If you're not qualified to treat the problem *without* hypnosis, then you're not qualified to treat the problem *with* hypnosis.

Tip #2: Define the therapeutic relationship clearly.

Tip #3: Define the relationship as active, collaborative and goal-oriented.

Tip #4: A quiet place to do hypnosis is very helpful, though not essential.

Tip #5: Furniture that fully supports someone as he or she relaxes is ideal since peoples' bodies often feel very heavy when relaxed.

Tip #6: Check for gum, candy, or anything else the client might accidentally choke on or swallow before beginning hypnosis.

Tip #7: Ask about previous experiences or exposures to hypnosis.

Tip #8: Consider carefully how your beliefs shape your therapeutic interactions.

Tip #9: Provide current and relevant information about hypnosis (psycho-education) to the client.

Tip #10: You don't need gimmicks and gadgets to do hypnosis. They are usually distracting and even cheesy.

Tip #11: Hypnosis lends itself too easily to making exaggerated claims about its merits. Don't make promises you can't keep.

Tip #12: Hypnosis lends itself too easily to "magical thinking." Do what you can to avoid reinforcing it in clinical applications.

Tip #13: No hypnosis technique is worth much if the client isn't able or willing to respond to it.

Tip #14: Don't just "trust the unconscious."

Tip #15: Find your own hypnotic voice and style.

Sales

& wealth will find you. 8-12-18 12:27AM

Tip #16: Understand the client's condition before you attempt to treat it.

Tip #17: Encourage action and independent solutions.

1. Planting the seed for loyalty
2. The sale happens when it nothing about the sale & everything about the client.
3. Make your sale great.
4. Selling to their silence
5. Take care of their trust & decision questions, it is where the path starts to the sale.

Tip #1 If you're not qualified to treat the problem *without* hypnosis, then you're not qualified to treat the problem *with* hypnosis.

Most people don't realize that to practice hypnosis in the majority of states in the U.S. or in other countries, there is no legal requirement to have an advanced academic degree, formal training from an approved educational provider, professional clinical licensure, or any special certification. Training programs in hypnosis can vary dramatically from the methods and concepts they teach to who is allowed to participate in the training. This lack of regulation can be confusing to people who want to be trained as well as those seeking the services of someone who provides treatment with hypnosis.

Thus, the field of hypnosis sometimes attracts people who know just enough to be dangerous. They may know a little about this or that, but not enough to provide well-informed and well-structured interventions that can prevent the kind of iatrogenic problems from arising when hypnosis is misapplied.

While some highly experienced and well-trained professionals can be plagued with self-doubt because they are acutely aware of how much there is to know in order to practice responsibly, others with far less training or understanding feel confident enough to make promises they cannot possibly keep. Is this a problem you can ethically and knowledgeably treat, or are you operating beyond your scope of expertise? It's a good idea to know your limits. With just a simple sentence, Dr. Martin Orne, a psychiatrist, researcher and hypnosis pioneer, established a common-sense guideline that is so critically important to all else, that it is my first tip: If you're not qualified to treat the problem *without* hypnosis, then you're not qualified to treat the problem *with* hypnosis.

Tip #2 Define the therapeutic relationship clearly.

From the time that a client calls to schedule a first appointment, the relationship between the clinician and the client begins to take shape. *How* it takes shape is an extremely important factor in the ways the relationship may ultimately become therapeutic or iatrogenic.

Some clinicians are much more formal and protocol bound in the way they define the relationship, others are more casual in the way they approach the treatment relationship. But, regardless of personal style and philosophy, there are specific standards that define the relationship as a clinical one rather than just a paid friendship. Every clinician must address the limits of confidentiality as well as the need for an informed consent to treatment on the part of the client.

Informed consent involves providing a discussion of available treatment options and why you recommend a specific treatment, what the expected benefit of the recommended treatment is based on empirical data, and what the liability might be of receiving no treatment at all. Beyond that, the clinician can speak to the roles that he or she as clinician and the client each play in the treatment process. How are their respective responsibilities defined? What is each expected to contribute to the treatment process? What are the parameters of the treatment right down to the details of costs, insurance coverage, scheduling of appointments, cancellation and no-show policies, telephone and electronic communications regarding sessions, and so on?

One of the related questions to this topic I am frequently asked in my trainings is, "How do you get your clients to do the homework assignments you give them?" There are a number of factors involved in my answer that go beyond the scope of this tip, but it starts with having defined the client's role as an active one in the therapy. Clients are informed from the start that I will ask them to do things on their behalf once we begin therapy. Setting the stage in this way helps define our relationship.

The more clearly the therapeutic relationship is defined, the less likelihood there is for miscommunication and subsequent difficulties. Clarity builds trust, trust builds an alliance, and an alliance builds greater hypnotic responsiveness.

Tip #3 Define the relationship as active, collaborative and goal-oriented.

Different therapeutic approaches define the client's role in treatment differently. Some treatments define the client's role as a passive one. For example, when antidepressants are prescribed as a sole form of treatment for depression, it transmits the unfortunate message, "You don't have to learn anything or change anything. You just need to take the drug and see if it works." Other treatments require the client to be more active in the process, perhaps carrying out structured experiments with new behaviors and perceptions or doing written assignments to promote a new awareness. The research evidence is clear that, in general, the more active the client is encouraged to be in treatment, the faster the rate and better the quality of results he or she will obtain.

Hypnosis is not practiced uniformly across practitioners. Some clinicians will define the client's role as a passive one by using techniques that invite the client to sit quietly with his or her eyes closed while the clinician reads a script or simply fires off suggestions to which the client is supposed to simply passively comply. This has been the traditional style of practice for a long time and many clinicians still practice in this style. In light of the evidence, encouraging a more active engagement on the part of the client is good practice.

In contrast to a passive approach, employing approaches to hypnosis that invite the client to be an active participant do at least two things differently than approaches that encourage passivity: 1) they interact with the client *during* the hypnosis session; and, 2) they require the client to actively process and even report on the relevance and significance of suggestions and make a determination as to how to integrate them.

Hypnosis is unapologetically a goal-oriented modality; every session has at least one objective and, ideally, both clinician and client are defined as active and collaborative agents working towards that objective. The goal-orientation reaffirms "we're here for a reason" and the expectation is that both partners are committed to producing a meaningful result. What a difference to do hypnosis *with* someone rather than *to* someone!

we have to be both charaters in the presentation & we both buy into the product.

Tip #4 A quiet place to do hypnosis is very helpful, though not essential.

If you have the ability to create an environment where you conduct your sessions, then you can make deliberate choices about what kind of environment you think would be helpful to your efforts. If there is little you can do to alter the environment in which you work, then you can adjust your hypnosis to the realities of that environment. While it is helpful to have a relatively quiet place in which to work, a lot of really great hypnosis is done routinely in environments that are far from ideal (such as emergency rooms and dental offices).

A quiet environment provides fewer distractions or disruptions to a client's ability to narrow his or her attention and focus on your input. But, attention is also mediated by how motivated the client is to pay attention as well as his or her quality of attention. Some people can get so focused as to fully tune out intruding distractions while absorbed in the hypnosis procedure even in unlikely environments. Some practitioners working in particularly noisy environments will even provide their clients with noise-canceling headphones and speak to them through a microphone that delivers the message more directly in a concentrated form through the headphones. This may be helpful but unnecessary depending on the quality of the client's attention.

Regardless of whatever environment you happen to work in, the salient skill to employ in hypnosis is utilizing the environment as a part of the hypnosis procedure. A suggestion such as, "Don't notice the noise" is a terrible one that immediately draws the person's attention to the noise. Furthermore, the word "noise" has negative connotations. A better suggestion might be, "As the routine sounds of the environment simply pass through your awareness, you can enjoy the feelings of comfort that grow more and more with each moment that passes." Even in a chaotic environment, the "sounds" can be defined as "routine" and therefore unnecessary to notice as "they simply pass through your awareness." Other suggestions such as, "When you get so comfortable and *quietly* absorbed, isn't it interesting how the rest of the world seems to just fade into the distance, the much *quieter* distance..." can be helpful. Good suggestions can usually compensate for bad environments.

Tip #5 Furniture that fully supports someone as he or she relaxes is ideal since peoples' bodies often feel very heavy when relaxed.

This may seem painfully obvious to you, but it's a factor many clinicians ask me about. If you do hypnosis regularly, it's helpful to have furniture that enhances the experience for your clients. When people start to relax, it is common for all or part of the body to feel quite heavy. This heaviness often translates into the hypnotic phenomenon called "catalepsy," defined as the inhibition of voluntary movement. Catalepsy can arise for different reasons, but when the body feels heavy and seems to require too much effort to move or reposition oneself, then a really comfortable chair that supports all of your body is wonderful to have.

When people get deeply absorbed in hypnosis and it takes too much effort to move, they may end up sitting too long in one position and end up with a neck ache from holding up their heavy head. Even though they could move and re-position themselves, of course, they sometimes don't.

As to what kind of furniture to have, it's a matter of personal opinion. Some clinicians will have clients lie down on a couch, while others view lying down as too vulnerable, or perhaps too sexually suggestive a position. Furthermore, a lying position may unintentionally invite the client, especially a tired client, to fall asleep during the hypnosis and thereby miss at least part of the session. My personal preference is a cushy chair that reclines just enough to provide leg support as well as head and neck support.

Tip #6 Check for gum, candy, or anything else the client might accidentally choke on or swallow before beginning hypnosis.

It is always a good idea to avoid unnecessary complications during the hypnosis session by thinking preventively regarding what might become an unwelcome intrusion. Whatever steps you can take to assure the client's safety and comfort should be taken.

One such step is making sure the client doesn't have anything in his or her mouth that could accidentally be swallowed. Unless you specifically ask, you could easily miss the fact that the client has something in his or her mouth. So, before you begin the session, ask the client about this or anything else that might interfere with his or her comfort once the session gets underway.

Tip #7 Ask about previous experiences or exposures to hypnosis.

Before you ever attempt hypnosis with someone, it should be a standard part of the interview process to ask about any previous hypnosis experiences. This might mean direct, personal experience with some other practitioner, or it might mean indirect exposures to hypnosis through someone else's reported experiences or through portrayals of hypnosis on television, in movies, or stage shows.

Questions B4 Starting

The reasons for asking are many:

1. If the person has had previous experience that was positive, the expectation of further positive experience aids treatment *if* what you do is consistent with (but not necessarily the same as) what was done before;

2. If the person's previous experience was negative, then knowing what was done before in detail prevents you from duplicating what the client regarded as a previous failure of hypnosis;

3. It may reveal misconceptions or unrealistic expectations about hypnosis the person may hold that might delay or even prevent positive treatment results if left uncorrected; and,

4. It provides an opportunity to explain the merits and describe the experience of hypnosis in such a way as to build cooperation and positive expectations for the hypnotic intervention to follow.

The research consistently shows that clients given some education about hypnosis have more realistic expectations and more satisfying hypnotic experiences. Describing how hypnosis feels, how natural and even routine it is in daily life (describing common examples such as so-called "highway hypnosis" the client can easily relate to), and how it can be therapeutic in general and personally beneficial to the client can help build receptivity. Knowing something about the client's history with hypnosis gives you the chance to make sure you and the client are both "on the same page" as treatment begins.

Tip #8 Consider carefully how your beliefs shape your therapeutic interactions.

How you think about people and what gives rise to their problems greatly influences the treatment philosophy and therapeutic orientation you adopt. Why one person becomes attracted to cognitive therapies and another to psychodynamic approaches and still another to biological approaches is much more a reflection of the person's values and beliefs than it is the merits of the therapy itself. After all, every therapy works with *someone* and for *some* problems. The wisdom is found in knowing which approach can be effective with *this* client for *this* problem. Thus, it is enormously valuable to do some self-exploration about how your values and beliefs influence your view of clients and their problems. To do this, you can pose all kinds of questions to yourself about why you think what you think and do what you do.

Some important questions might include the following:

1. Of all the factors – biological, psychological, and social – that feature in any problem, why focus on the factor(s) you are inclined to focus upon and downplay others that other clinicians might view as primary?

2. Do you believe the goal of therapy is to reduce pathology or expand wellness, and what are the implications of your answer in terms of your clinical approach?

3. Do you believe people want or need to suffer or they're doing the best they can with the resources they have?

4. Do you believe people can be cured of nearly everything if you just approach treatment in the "right" way? and,

5. What do you believe about hypnosis and its role in therapy?

The number and type of questions you can ask yourself to clarify your beliefs and values relative to your role as a clinician are nearly infinite. The clarity that emerges from such questioning is one of the most important characteristics of great clinicians.

Tip #9 Provide current and relevant information about hypnosis (psycho-education) to the client.

As mentioned above, the research makes it clear that it helps the therapeutic effort to have a client who is reasonably well informed about the treatment in general, and especially when a potentially misunderstood tool such as hypnosis is to be employed. Thus, prior to beginning the use of hypnosis, there can be a discussion about hypnosis. It doesn't have to be a long discussion, by any means, but enough to make it clear why you're recommending hypnosis, what the client can expect to experience during hypnosis, and anything else that might be helpful to the interaction. It is particularly important to emphasize this is not something you do *to* him or her. Rather, it is something you do *with* him or her.

There are some clinicians who use the psychoeducational opportunity to talk about the myths and misconceptions about hypnosis, and raise all the fears and doubts about hypnosis without the client ever having professed to be plagued by such fears or doubts. There's no reason to just launch into a lecture about myths and misconceptions until you've gotten feedback from the client that he or she actually holds some of them.

I much prefer to use everyday examples of absorption, such as when watching a compelling movie or reading a great book that leads you into a selfless focus, easy examples of being both self-aware and deeply absorbed that reflect hypnotic experiences well. The emphasis is on being wrapped up in what's going on, yet still aware and in control, able to end the absorption at will. The more you describe hypnosis as a natural experience rather than a magical one, the better treatment response you are likely to get. Furthermore, the more you emphasize how much of therapy involves learning and that people learn better when they're relaxed and focused, the better the rationale you provide for pursuing experience with hypnosis on a realistic and collaborative basis.

Tip #10 You don't need gimmicks and gadgets to do hypnosis. They are usually distracting and even cheesy.

There is a wide array of things that people will do in the name of hypnosis, incorporating gimmicky objects or elaborate and dramatic moves into their procedures. Most people are familiar with the swinging pendulum, rhythmic metronome and swirling hypnosis spirals, all of which are superfluous to the hypnotic experience. In addition to these common tactics, some people also use flashing, blinking or swirling lights, making dramatic sweeping arm gestures, touching the client's forehead, standing behind the client and rocking or otherwise moving him or her in unusual ways, making peculiar hand movements, staring and even intimidating the client with their unwavering gaze, introducing special smells (such as baby powder for doing a regression), using an exaggeratedly fast rate of speech or monotonous tone of voice, employing a special machine to create hypnotic brain waves, and many other such gadgets and gimmicks to ostensibly generate the experience of hypnosis.

Not only are these entirely unnecessary and generally undesirable in conducting clinical hypnosis sessions, they can be and usually are counterproductive. They unintentionally reinforce the "magical" view of hypnosis as outside the realm of "normal" experience. They suggest you need some gadget or gimmick in order for hypnosis to occur, and thereby place less emphasis on the quality of the hypnotic interaction between clinician and client that is the foundation for effective hypnosis. They further reinforce the unfortunate notions that hypnosis is something done *to* you rather than *with* you and that hypnosis is strange as are the people who practice hypnosis, evidenced by the dramatic and even weird way they act when performing their craft.

Engaging the client in a caring relationship that is respectful and supportive means leaving the drama and the gimmicks out of the process. Instead, the focus should be on inviting a thoughtful collaboration with the client in a serious therapeutic process.

Tip #11 Hypnosis lends itself too easily to making exaggerated claims about its merits. Don't make promises you can't keep.

It's important for people to have positive expectations about the treatment they're receiving. Positive expectations can lead people to align their behaviors, consciously and unconsciously, with the treatment goals and thereby add another helpful ingredient to the process. But, how far can you go in encouraging positive expectations before you cross a line and encourage people to believe in unrealistic expectations? It's a sensitive issue for people who practice hypnosis, especially those professionals who are unwilling to make exaggerated claims for the "power of hypnosis" that some practitioners don't hesitate to make.

PART 2

Over the decades, the things I have seen people promise through their phone book (remember phone books?) and newspaper ads and now through their websites and *YouTube* videos have too often been nothing short of outrageous. This is one of the factors that clearly distinguish ethical and sensible practitioners from those that are comfortable saying almost anything to hook in gullible clients. The promises people make can range from "instant pain relief" to "hypnotically healing cancer" to "rapid self-esteem."

What type of practitioner advertises promises they can't possibly keep? *Anyone* can do this, of course, but such promises are far more likely to be made by people who don't carefully consider what is reasonable to lead a client to believe. What complicates the issue is the fact that sometimes people *do* generate some wonderfully surprising, almost miraculous, results. Even so, how can someone *promise* such a result? Can we take the extraordinary things that some people can do and then suggest to someone that, "since this is humanly possible because so-and-so did it, you can do it, too?" Here's another belief in yourself to clarify: Do you believe anyone can do anything if they just have the right attitude or the right hypnotic suggestion? I hope not. It's a potentially very dangerous belief to hold as it sets people up to fail with predictably negative consequences. After all, no matter how motivated a client might be to see the sunset, he or she won't see it by looking to the east. Motivation without ability means little, as does ability without motivation. Exaggerated promises may be good for business, but they're bad for people.

Tip #12 Hypnosis lends itself too easily to "magical thinking." Do what you can to avoid reinforcing it in clinical applications.

If you go to *YouTube* and type the word "hypnosis" into the search engine, you will find endless videos featuring people using hypnosis to regress you to past lives, relive your birth, feel high as if you smoked marijuana or took LSD, meet your spirit animal guide, attract instant wealth, travel out of your body to distant places, meet your guardian angel, remember being abducted by extraterrestrial visitors from another galaxy, and on and on. What is it about hypnosis that leads people to use it for such esoteric and even bizarre purposes?

One way of thinking about hypnosis is as an amplifier of subjective experience. The basic principle "what you focus on you amplify" can yield some especially unusual and dramatic responses when you amplify peoples' most idiosyncratic beliefs and perceptions. People are capable of believing all kinds of things that may have nothing to do with objective reality, a phenomenon that relates to what clinicians call "magical thinking," the belief in imagined relationships (such as a broken mirror causing seven years bad luck or having to wear your "lucky socks" to the game or else your team won't win). These beliefs generally reflect a lack of critical thinking skills. They may be harmless or they may be the basis for some of the most distressing symptoms and experiences imaginable.

Hypnosis was described by two very prominent researchers in the field, psychologists Ted Sarbin and Ernest Hilgard, as "believed-in imagination," a phrase that captures an important aspect of hypnosis. People in hypnosis can voluntarily set aside objective reality and immerse themselves in a suggested reality that they then respond to as if real. So, as an example, when someone is regressed to a so-called past life, he or she might have an emotionally dramatic and perceptually detailed experience of being in that distant era doing those things. But, this is entirely subjective, an amplification of pre-existing beliefs in or openness to reincarnation that lend themselves to this kind of experience.

When they re-orient after the experience, they may feel "enlightened" about their past lives, and even feel these provided therapeutic benefit, now that they "know where the symptom came from." But, this is magical thinking, leading someone to believe karma is to blame for their problems instead of their own experiences or bad decisions in this life.

Esoteric applications of hypnosis based only on the shared idiosyncratic beliefs of the clinician and client rarely, if ever, have a place in sensible therapies. The stale argument that some people get better from such approaches is terribly weak given that there are many, many other ways to achieve the same therapeutic objectives *without* encouraging magical thinking or misrepresenting hypnosis.

It is important to clarify that this tip relates to how you use hypnosis in an ethical clinical practice. It is not a statement about what you choose to believe in regards to past life regressions or any of the other phenomena mentioned. It is one thing to have a personal belief but quite another to bring it into the therapy room.

Tip #13 No hypnosis technique is worth much if the client isn't able or willing to respond to it.

The earlier consideration of words as triggers for subjective experience highlighted the vitally important point that the meaning isn't in the word itself. Rather, the meaning is in the person's subjective interpretation of the word. Similarly, the hypnosis techniques you employ provide a means for generating subjective experiences in the client that are triggered by the larger framework in which the technique is embedded. You have a therapeutic goal, you choose a strategy thought to be a means of attaining the goal, and the hypnosis then proceeds. As established earlier, hypnotic responsiveness is mediated by personal, interpersonal and contextual variables. The context for hypnosis represents the broadest array of variables, encompassing such key factors as how the client's problem is conceptualized, how the therapeutic targets are identified, how the unique attributes of the client are taken into consideration when planning the treatment, how the treatment will be implemented, how methods will be adjusted according to client feedback, and how progress will be evaluated.

A hazard in providing treatment is providing a wrong or merely ineffective treatment. What makes a treatment "wrong" or "ineffective?" Consider this: When a clinician goes to a workshop to learn new clinical techniques and becomes convinced in the merits of some new approach, he or she may go back to work and use the new technique, only to discover that what worked so well at the workshop is not working at all with this particular client. Why not? There was something about the context, as well as the personal and interpersonal factors present with this client, that precluded the technique from working. What was the structure of the technique? What did it amplify, or *attempt* to amplify, in the client's experience? It can take some time to unravel and identify these factors, but this needs to be done to minimize the chance of future episodes of no or poor results. No one succeeds all the time, of course, highlighting the point that the technique you use isn't where the power is. The power is in the client's ability to respond to the technique. *No* technique is going to succeed if the context doesn't support its use.

Tip #14 Don't just "trust the unconscious."

Modern cognitive neuroscientists study complex mental phenomena. They don't typically refer to "*the* unconscious" anymore as if it is a discrete and organized entity. Rather, they refer to "unconscious processes" that influence perception and behavior. What cognitive neuroscience reveals about mental functioning is that people don't have a single, unified consciousness. Nor do we simply have a conscious mind and an unconscious mind. In fact, we have multiple cognitive systems that function simultaneously, arranged in a hierarchy under the control of what is termed an "executive system." The executive system is responsible for deliberating and forming intentional responses. But non-conscious cognitive systems that involve emotion, motivation, goals, self-regulation, and biases all influence the choices we make and the responses we form without our knowing where the unconscious influences come from.

Scientists study the effects of "priming," a process of exposing people to words, images, or objects outside of conscious awareness, then exposing them to some task or situation where the unconscious influence may be seen to affect their responses. One simple example is when a group of people work together on a problem-solving task; just having a briefcase on the table rather than a backpack leads people to act more competitively without knowing why. Priming achievement goals, as typically occurs in therapy, has been shown to improve task performance, increase peoples' creativity, increase their ability to stay on task, increase the strength of their desire to complete the task, and even more flexibly adjust their responses when the task rules change. So, one way of thinking about hypnosis is as a process of priming client responses. But, this is a variable process, neither consistent nor predictable, and so can't simply be "trusted."

While it is purely a myth that "hypnosis bypasses conscious analysis and hypnotic suggestions go directly into the unconscious," suggestions can be viewed as having priming characteristics that *may* influence unconscious processes. Thus, those hypnosis practitioners who promote the idea that if you can just "get the suggestion into the client's unconscious" you can "trust the unconscious" to absorb it and use it are misrepresenting what actually occurs. Likewise, when practitioners make use of metaphorical approaches during hypnosis and the meaning of the story is purposely ambiguous, there is no legitimate basis for believing that "the client's unconscious will derive the intended meaning." "Trusting the unconscious" is blind faith in cognitive processes that cannot be predicted or influenced in any terms other than general ones. Well-formed suggestions may have an impact… but maybe not.

Tip #15 Find your own hypnotic voice and style.

Each of us learns hypnosis from those that we consider experts. These are the people that demonstrate hypnotic techniques, conduct illustrative hypnosis sessions, and generally inform us about how hypnosis "should" be done. It is natural to want to emulate those instructors and clinicians we consider to be knowledgeable and experienced, not only adopting their techniques but even adopting their posture, tone of voice and delivery. However, as discussed previously, emulating someone else's style suggests that his or her approach is the "right" one and the power is in his or her suggestions and style. But, that's not true. You can offer a client the same suggestions and imitate the style of delivery you learned from someone, but still get a poor response simply because that approach didn't fit for that client.

Therapeutic success still comes down to clinical judgment and the unique relationship between you and your client. If the relationship and the rest of the contextual factors don't support the use of a particular approach, then it really doesn't matter that you saw it succeed when someone else applied that technique with someone else in some other circumstance. It's so important to come to the realization that other people can get responses from people you can't get – but *you* can get responses from people *they* can't get. Your personality, your way of looking at things, your way of inspiring confidence, and your way of showing that you care are all factors that can define you as worth listening to. Learning to use your voice and body in ways that amplify your message is part of evolving your individual style. Developing ways to structure your sessions and make choices about how to present ideas to your clients, as well as the words and gestures you'll use in doing hypnosis sessions, are also part of evolving your individual style.

There isn't a right way to do hypnosis. There are *lots* of right ways, so it would be great if you found *yours*.

Tip #16 Understand the client's condition before you attempt to treat it.

When people first learn hypnosis and begin to use it, the results can sometimes seem nothing short of miraculous. The ability to reduce peoples' symptoms, physical and emotional, can lead some practitioners to believe they have special powers that they can use to cure anybody of almost anything. The enthusiasm for hypnosis is wonderful, but the level of confidence bubbling up in some people who just finished their first hypnosis courses is worrisome. This overconfidence in hypnosis and in oneself can too easily give rise to making outrageously exaggerated claims for one's abilities. Beyond these, it can lead practitioners to believe that all they have to do is "hypnotize away" the client's symptoms. Their unjustified self-confidence in using hypnosis can easily lead them to unhesitatingly treat conditions they don't really know much about.

The old saying, "Fools rush in where angels fear to tread" applies here. Furthermore, the wisdom of Martin Orne's ethical guideline, "If you're not qualified to treat the problem *without* hypnosis, then you're not qualified to treat the problem *with* hypnosis" is worth repeating. What I'm speaking to here is how believing you know more than you really do can too easily lead you to offer suggestions in hypnosis that make things worse for the client, not better. This can be true when addressing psychological problems, such as anxiety or depression, where you focus the client on ideas that are inconsistent with overcoming these problems. For example, one might think that "depression is anger turned inward" (an obsolete yet persistent view), and therefore this client needs to "get the suppressed anger out." So, you prescribe pounding a chair with a pillow, oblivious to the abundance of research that shows unambiguously that focusing people on their anger makes them angry, *not* better.

A current and empirically informed view of depression is necessary for proper treatment. Similarly, if you have a distressed client who suffers with symptoms from MS (multiple sclerosis), you might think it potentially helpful to offer suggestions for relaxing by a pool or at the beach, soaking up the warmth of the sun. Then, to your unhappy surprise, the client begins to have muscle spasms because you didn't know that heat aggravates MS symptoms. Before you attempt to treat someone with (or without) hypnosis, it is imperative that you have enough understanding of the condition you hope to treat so that you don't inadvertently offer suggestions that are counter-productive.

Tip #17 Encourage action and independent solutions.

Providing suggestions for relaxing imagery can be a valuable way to promote greater comfort in a distressed or anxious client. However, clients can *feel* better without actually *being* better. When there are suggestions given for taking action, especially *specific* actions, that empower the client to be proactive, there is a much better chance the client will actually take the suggested actions.

Even if the client doesn't take the specific actions you suggest, but then takes different actions that still generate improvement, your suggestions were a catalyst for facilitating those client-generated actions. Clients don't necessarily need to comply with your suggestions to the letter. They can reply to your suggestions with solutions they generated themselves in response to your suggestions. This is an even better outcome because of the independence they asserted on their own behalf. Help them bring out their Answers.

Using hypnosis to encourage more flexible thinking and behaving, and encouraging clients to approach problems by doing something different rather than just trying the same thing harder, are some of the best uses of hypnosis. We want to encourage action, we want to encourage *different* actions, and we want to encourage greater independence as problem-solving skills evolve.

Absorb the meaning of this relevant metaphor: Give someone a fish and you've given him or her a meal. Teach someone how to fish and you've given him or her a livelihood.

Part 3:

Tips for Designing Hypnosis Sessions

Tips for Designing Hypnosis Sessions

In this section, I turn your attention to tips for building hypnosis sessions that feature both insight and foresight. In doing so, I am clearly encouraging having a well thought out plan for the session before it begins. It isn't enough to just "wing it" or tell the client a story you hope will connect. I, like other experienced clinicians who eschew scripted approaches, prefer to have the freedom to be spontaneous in conducting sessions. But, I also know that it's essential to do some pre-planning if the session is going to have well defined objectives and provide the client with meaningful direction. The plan also includes what to do when you have to deviate from the plan because of some unexpected issue or response that arises.

It's an old insurance sales pitch, but it's true nonetheless: *People don't plan to fail. They fail to plan.*

List of Tips for Designing Hypnosis Sessions

Tip #18: Define problems in ways that make them solvable.

Tip #19: What you focus on, you amplify. Consider carefully what you want to amplify in the client's experience, and why.

Tip #20: Identifying hypnotic phenomena evident in the client's symptoms can inform your treatment plan.

Tip #21: Not everyone is capable of focusing well. You may want to spend some time striving to build focus before you attempt to use that focus in a goal-oriented hypnosis session.

Tip #22: Record your hypnosis sessions.

Tip #23: A hypnosis session can only be effective when it hits the salient target.

Tip #24: People are much more than their labels.

Tip #25: The hypnotic induction you use doesn't matter, except that it does.

Tip #26: Structure sessions to progress from general to specific.

Tip #27: Structure sessions to go from less to more emotionally charged.

Tip #28: The greater the resistance, the greater the need for indirection.

Tip #29: Promote uncertainty to build responsiveness.

Tip #30: Often, the people who most need the experience of hypnosis are the ones who are most afraid of it.

Tip #31: If the client has difficulty closing his or her eyes, then do the hypnosis session with his or her eyes open.

Tip #32: Avoid duplicating techniques that the client associates with failure.

Tip #33: Hypnosis is not a lie detector or a means to discover "the truth."

Tip #34: Don't believe a memory is true just because it's detailed or emotional.

Tip #35: Affect can be dissociated, so beware of the "I've got a feeling" trap.

Tip #36: Make use of presuppositions to build expectancy.

Tip #37: Expand the client's sensory experience during hypnosis.

Tip #38: People differ in the degree of amnesia they may experience following hypnosis.

Tip #39: You can re-traumatize someone by revivifying a traumatic memory.

Tip #40: Focusing each session on trauma or other deeply painful issues can be counterproductive.

Tip #41: Do your best to prevent the session from ending on a negative.

Tip #18 Define problems in ways that make them solvable.

The diverse ways that clinicians have of looking at the same problem is fascinating. A room full of clinicians can all simultaneously hear the same story from a client about the problems he or she is facing, and the different and even opposing views they generate in response are amazing. Amazing, but *not* surprising.

Every client who walks in the door asking for help is a complex entity with many different facets. Complex people and ambiguous circumstances naturally invite projections as we strive to make meaning out of the ambiguity. If you're familiar with the *Rorschach Inkblot Test,* then you know you show the test subject an inkblot, a purposely ambiguous stimulus, and ask him or her what he or she "sees" in the inkblot. What else can people do but use their own frame of reference and projections to make sense out of the ambiguous stimulus?

Metaphorically speaking, every client we see is a walking inkblot, so it is hardly a surprise when different clinicians see the same client's problems from different frames of reference and want to treat that person from their perspective. Since the same problem can be seen from so many different perspectives, how do we evaluate the merits of any one clinician's perspective, especially when there can be so many "right" ways to look at a client's problem?

One factor to consider is whether the clinician's perspective defines the client's problem in solvable or unsolvable terms. The clinical world is a world of fads and fashions, easily swayed by the treatment model or clinical phrase that's the popular one right now. Clinicians subscribe to different viewpoints and these become their frame of reference for making clinical decisions. But, some frames of reference make it harder to treat the problem effectively. If a clinician says, "This problem runs in your family so it must be genetic," does that define the problem as changeable? If a clinician says, "You're suffering now because you're an ACA, the Adult Child of an Alcoholic," does that indicate the problem is changeable? If you are, in fact, an ACA, how exactly do you stop that? If a clinician says, "Your problems stem from your traumatic history," how does an *unchangeable history* help define the problems as changeable?

Clinicians have to be careful to use language in ways that emphasize malleability if they're going to be in the business of promoting change.

Tip #19 What you focus on, you amplify. Consider carefully what you want to amplify in the client's experience, and why.

If I suggest to you that you focus on your left foot, which I'd guess just came into your awareness, you now have an amplified awareness for your left foot. I can further amplify it by asking questions about your left foot: is it resting on the floor or is it elevated because you're reclining right now or perhaps because your left leg is crossed over your right? Are you barefoot or are you wearing a shoe? Every suggestion you provide and every question you ask inevitably amplifies *something* in your client's experience. How do you decide which aspect of a client's experience you want to amplify? This question addresses the foundation on which you build your hypnosis session.

The goals that you set for a hypnosis session naturally reflect what you think is important, and what you think is important is reflected in the theory or theories you subscribe to and the techniques derived from them. If you believe that the so-called "cognitive distortions" (errors in thinking) are the basis for the client's problems, then using hypnosis to introduce a more accurate way of thinking would make perfect sense to you. Likewise, if you believe that the client's lack of emotional awareness is the reason for his or her difficulties, then using hypnosis to promote a greater recognition of and ability to label and articulate feelings would seem the "right" approach.

Every therapy focuses on one aspect of a client's experience or another, amplifying it in the client's awareness in the process. As an example, consider cognitive-behavioral therapy (CBT) and its relevance to treating someone who is emotionally overwhelmed with depression or anxiety. A question I am often asked at my workshops on treating depression is, "Dr. Yapko, don't you think it's important to help a depressed individual get in touch with his or her feelings?" Well, what do you *think* he or she is in touch with? Would *more* focus on depressed feelings really be therapeutic? CBT teaches people how to get *out* of their feelings and focus on the facts in order to make better, more rational decisions. It is no surprise, then, that so many clinicians around the world think of CBT as the treatment of choice for depression and anxiety.

The point, of course, is that a clinician has to really think through how to structure the hypnosis session to amplify those aspects of the client's experience that will be the most likely to catalyze positive results. Treatment can't just be the same for everybody, whether with hypnosis scripts or a single treatment modality.

Tip #20 Identifying hypnotic phenomena evident in the client's symptoms can inform your treatment plan.

The so-called classical hypnotic phenomena (such as age regression, age progression, anesthesia, catalepsy, dissociation, positive and negative hallucinations, time distortion, etc.) represent the building blocks of human experience. They are *neutral* in their potential, equally capable of being used in both positive and negative ways. They can be structured to be therapeutic in clinical hypnosis sessions, or they can evolve as negative coping devices that result in distressing symptoms.

Consider hypnotic anesthesia as an example. To use hypnosis to help people suffering with physical pain to reduce or even eliminate their pain so they can resume a normal life is a fantastic and compassionate use of hypnosis. But, at the other end of the anesthesia spectrum, there is the client who takes a knife and intentionally slices his or her arm in a well-practiced "cutting" behavior. Shocked, you ask, "Doesn't that hurt?" Even more shocking is the answer: "No, it doesn't hurt. It's how I get my feelings out. It feels *good.*" It can be quite an insight to realize that the same hypnotic phenomena you study for therapeutic purposes are structurally the same as those used by clients for generating symptoms.

As you interview your client and start to get some understanding of what this individual is currently experiencing and what the goals are in coming to see you, it can be quite helpful to consider what role hypnotic experiences may be playing in the formation of their symptoms. By knowing how the client's symptoms may be utilizing hypnotic phenomena, you will be better able to counterbalance your hypnotic suggestions. For example, the absorption in past hurts (viewable as the "uncontrolled age regressions" depressed people typically do to stay "stuck in the past") needs to be counterbalanced by a positive orientation to the future through structured age *progressions.* Similarly, the physical *dissociation* that permits poisoning yourself with cigarettes needs to be counterbalanced with an amplified connection (*association*) to your body as well as a protective attitude towards it that precludes a willingness to smoke. The larger point is that what makes hypnosis potentially valuable in treatment is having a deeper understanding of *how* the client generates symptomatic experiences with hypnosis and *how* the hypnosis you do as a clinician can amplify experiences that will counterbalance them.

Tip #21 Not everyone is capable of focusing well. You may want to spend some time striving to build focus before you attempt to use that focus in a goal-oriented hypnosis session.

There are many different conditions that feature an impairment to people's ability to pay attention. Attention Deficit Hyperactivity Disorder (ADHD) is an obvious example. There are also many other disorders that involve difficulty focusing, such as depression, anxiety and pain, to name a few.

Beyond diagnosable clinical problems, a difficulty paying attention is exacerbated by the influence of today's technology. One Microsoft executive described it well when she coined the phrase, "continuous partial attention" to describe the ever-present distractions from text messages, email, phone calls, news programs that also feature a "crawl" on the bottom of the screen providing written news while we're also watching and listening to the main newscast. The net effect is to have a negative impact on peoples' ability to focus, which, of course, affects their ability to be hypnotized.

As you interview or treat clients, the qualities of their attention should be among the first things you make a point of assessing. This encompasses their quality of focus (whether more or less diffuse), direction of focus (whether more internal or externally absorbed), and recognition of saliency (whether they notice what truly matters or get distracted by irrelevancies). Your observations of the client's attentional style will inform your approach to the client.

One of the good things that can come out of hypnosis for clients with a limited attention span is a deliberate building of focus as a preliminary to the other things you intend to do in therapy. When you do short and progressively longer inductions multiple times within a single session, a technique called "fractionation" by some and "refractionation" by others, you're helping to build a greater attention span. You want the client to be focused and engaged before you start delivering strong therapeutic messages. To deliver such messages when the person isn't yet capable of paying sufficient attention to them is a sure way to frustrate both you and your client.

Tip #22 Record your hypnosis sessions.

One of the best tools you have available to you to help achieve your therapeutic objectives is the ability to record your hypnosis sessions. Digital recording technologies have made recording sessions easier than ever and produce higher quality recordings than ever before.

When you conduct a hypnosis session in your office, clients are in your space, not theirs. They're also in a particular frame of mind and body at the time. When they have the opportunity to be in their own space and listen to and experience the same session again from the recording, it is *guaranteed* that they will hear things they didn't hear before and react to things they didn't even notice before.

The value of the hypnosis recordings includes:

1. A chance for the client to re-listen to the suggestions and reinforce their strength and impact, thereby building therapeutic momentum;

2. A structured means for clients to repeat and practice going into hypnosis in at least two different contexts (your office and their home) and thereby increasing their potential for building greater comfort and hypnotic responsiveness:

3. A record of the session in case you want to review what you said and how you said it if and when the client reports improvement (or the opposite) or tells you how important what you said was even when you don't remember saying it; and,

4. A confidence-building measure of therapeutic progress if and when a client listens to the recording from, say, a month ago, and the recording is no longer relevant because what was a concern then has been resolved and is no longer a concern.

It's a good idea as per number three above to keep a copy of your recordings before you give the client a copy. It's also wise to have clients sign a statement assuming responsibility for the recording once you provide it to them.

The American Society of Clinical Hypnosis (ASCH) provides useful guidelines for electronic recordings of hypnosis on their website (www.asch.net). Clinicians are also encouraged to review the HIPAA laws and guidelines for protecting client confidentiality.

Tip #23 A hypnosis session can only be effective when it hits the salient target.

There are many different reasons why a hypnosis session can fall flat. Perhaps the most common reason is because the session's target was either incorrectly or too vaguely defined. This represents one of the most powerful ways in which clinicians differ from one another. How one clinician sees the client's problem and how to best address it can be light years away from how another clinician views and would treat that same problem.

Consider a client who wants to quit smoking cigarettes. One clinician emphasizes the power of nicotine addiction ("it's worse than heroin") and the grueling process of physical withdrawal and ways to manage it. Another clinician emphasizes the situational cues that trigger smoking behavior such as drinking in a bar or scheduled work breaks and prescribes changing the behavioral routine to "short-circuit the triggers." Still another clinician focuses on cigarettes as "your friend" and prepares the client for the "grieving process you will need to go through for the loss of this friendship."

These represent very different approaches to the treatment of smoking based on markedly different assumptions. Which approach, if *any*, is more likely to "hit the mark" and make it easier for someone to stop smoking? For a specific client, one approach may be helpful but another seemingly plausible approach results in total failure. This issue is so important I address it in great detail in my recent book, *The Discriminating Therapist*. In that book, I address and help clinicians work through the thorny issue of how to provide effective treatment without interpreting the "meaning" of someone's symptoms. Instead of asking the usual question "why" someone has the problem and thereby merely invite speculation, I focus on the structure of the problem by asking *"how"* the person generates their symptoms.

The focus on *how* the person generates his or her symptoms yields insights into the steps he or she follows to end up in distress. In this way, the clinician can learn the sequence the client follows, and through therapy and the hypnosis that's part of the therapy, can then introduce interruptions to that sequence. Therapy, *any* therapy, has to get people to stop doing what they're doing and do something else. Hence, therapy can be described as a process of *pattern interruption* and *pattern building*. The skill is in knowing *which* patterns to interrupt and how to build more adaptive ones. It works against accuracy in defining the target, though, when the target is associated to some theoretical construct the clinician just happens to believe in or is defined in over-general terms (such as "this is a self-esteem problem").

Tip #24 People are much more than their labels.

The traditional medical model that has permeated the health care professions in America (and lots of other places, too) mandates making a diagnosis first and then formulating a treatment. This makes perfect sense in physical medicine, of course. But, in the mental health domain, the medical model loses some of its value for at least two reasons:

First, mental health problems shouldn't automatically be considered "mental diseases." As an example, let's consider the disorder of Major Depressive Disorder, or more simply, depression. When depression so often arises from broader *social conditions* such as poverty and racism, and from *social causes* such as bullying, loss of loved ones, physical or sexual abuse at the hands of another person, humiliation, rejection, and so on, does the label "disease" apply? More important, in such instances, does the disease label give rise to any better a quality of treatment?

Second, the diagnosing of mental health problems can be an unreliable process. Psychiatric diagnoses are generally more subjective than medical diagnoses, yet once the diagnostic label has been given to the client it is likely to stick even if it isn't accurate.

Unfortunately, as clinicians we are trained to look for and therefore naturally find our clients' weaknesses or pathologies when they come to us for treatment. In so doing, we miss a chance to discover their strengths and innate resources. This is one of the things I appreciate most about the practice of clinical hypnosis: it begins with the unwavering belief that clients have more strengths and resources than they realize or use. Knowing that people are more than a diagnostic label makes it possible to *look for what more they are.* Although an individual might be depressed, he or she has valuable skills such as fixing things in need of repair, bringing comfort to others who are suffering, or playing one helluva banjo. The person is more than his or her depression and a goal is to amplify what's *right* with this person.

In this way, the practice of hypnosis is a type of applied "positive psychology," a growing force in the mental health field that has come to the realization that the focus on pathology throughout the history of psychotherapy has not made us collectively better. So, positive psychology asks bigger questions such as, how can we inspire the best in people? How can we encourage compassion, generosity, selflessness and other character strengths and virtues? The belief in the potential of humans to be better is actualized in hypnosis sessions that focus on the strengths rather than weaknesses.

Tip #25 The hypnotic induction you use doesn't matter, except that it does.

Virtually anything that captures and holds the client's attention can be utilized as an induction. If you hold up a glass of water and start talking about its clarity and your musings as to whether the glass is half empty or half full, and the client can get absorbed in that verbiage, then you've done an apparently successful "glass of water induction." Since an induction can take an infinite variety of forms, ranging from structured to conversational, how do you decide which induction to employ?

On one level, which specific induction you choose to use really doesn't matter. What matters is that the client is engaged and responds to it. On another level, though, which induction you use matters *a lot*. After all, the induction is the beginning of establishing a structure and style for the session, providing an early orientation as to how the session will unfold. Thus, the larger aims of the hypnosis session should be a major factor to consider in determining your approach to the induction. Of course, what one clinician would choose to emphasize may be quite different than what another clinician might choose.

If you know, for example, that you're going to be doing a hypnosis session designed to provide pain relief to your client, then you also know that your larger therapeutic strategy will likely involve some physical dissociation, encouraging a sense of detachment from the body or just the painful parts of the body. If you're going to be doing physical dissociation in the main part of the session, then would you employ an induction like a progressive muscle relaxation or body scan that focuses on relaxing the body? No, to *amplify* an awareness of the body, a physically *associative* strategy, when the goal is to encourage a physical *dissociation*, will be counter-productive. Instead, the induction needs to be one that is in line with encouraging dissociation and begins that way. For example, you might begin the induction by saying, "When you close your eyes… the way you have now… it can make it so easy to begin to experience a *wonderful distance*… from the usual cues… the world just seems to *slip away*... and you can experience all the comfort of your body sitting in the chair... while your thoughts and imagination allow you to *be somewhere else* entirely..." The seeds for the fuller dissociation(s) to come are being planted in the induction. Here is yet another example of the limitations of scripted approaches; it makes a big difference in client responsiveness whether you're saying, in essence, "here's my impersonal induction technique, now respond to it," or you're saying, "here are ideas to focus you on what matters to you as an individual." Which approach to use will, of course, be based on how you think about using hypnosis.

Tip #26 Structure sessions to progress from general to specific.

One of the most valuable technical tips I can offer concerns not hitting the client too hard too quickly with input that is too personal or too challenging. When you design a hypnosis session, the first consideration is being clear about what you want to tell the client. What's the therapeutic message you hope to convey? If you can't articulate this message succinctly and clearly and have some certainty about its importance to the client's therapy, then the hypnosis session is unlikely to be of much value. But, once you are clear about your message, it now becomes a question of how to build the client's receptivity to that message. As you know, the mere fact that the person is in hypnosis is hardly a guarantee the person will absorb and use your message. So, it becomes an important procedural step to move gradually from a general discussion of the relevant point to a more specific path for the client to apply that point in his or her own behalf.

As an example, before you talk to the client about the changes he or she can or should make, you can absorb the client in your descriptions of the "inevitability of changes" across our lifespan, first in impersonal terms. Describing the changes in technology that will be unfolding in the years to come, and the social changes that will come about as a result, and other such *impersonal* examples, all orient the client in a general and non-threatening way first to the notion of "change as inevitable." After all, there's no legitimate basis for denying that technological and social changes will occur. Then you can be a little more specific - but still general - when you describe the changes *all* people go through as they age and acquire more diverse experiences and establish new relationships and reach goals and set new ones and so forth. Finally, you can be more specific and personal about that client's successful changes in the past and the resources he or she has that made them possible. Then you can move on to acknowledge he or she is now in a new phase of life with new goals and how he or she can use previously established resources as well as find new resources that can be mobilized to achieve what he or she came to therapy to achieve. This is an example of going from general to specific and building a momentum for change gradually that fosters fuller and better responses to hypnosis.

Tip #27 Structure sessions to go from less to more emotionally charged.

Just as we want the session to build a conceptual momentum by going from general to specific, we also want to build an emotional momentum by going from less to more emotionally charged material as the session progresses. When clients have been suffering with their problems for some length of time, perhaps months or even years, there is often an accumulation of frustration and self-criticism stemming from all the unsuccessful attempts to resolve the problems and all the stress that has built up around the issues. The client can be stewing in some pretty intense emotions and getting these into a meaningful perspective can be a therapeutic challenge.

Typically, a hypnosis session will address a number of different themes or topics that represent core components of the client's difficulties. For example, you may want to say something to the client about developing clearer and stronger personal boundaries in order to better manage some destructive relationship. Addressing the boundary issue in specific ways with a toxic person the client has not managed well is likely to bring up some strong feelings of hurt, anger, resentment, grief, and more. The session needs to build up to that by starting in a less charged area. So, the first part of the session might involve speaking generally about how people are "wired" to be social and the different social roles each person plays (at once a son or daughter, husband or wife, mom or dad, employee or employer, etc.). This isn't an emotionally charged topic, but it starts the client thinking about roles he or she occupies.

Next, you can talk about what defines the role, the behaviors that you must engage in according to the demands of the role, as well as the behaviors you cannot engage in to fulfill that role. This is a little more emotionally charged, but still not too personal. Then you can make it much more personal describing where the boundaries are that define a role in an intimate relationship and what happens when one person crosses the line and the other doesn't do anything about it. Here comes the emotionalism and it rides in on the recognition that boundaries are essential, knowing where your boundaries are is important and protecting them is a never ending personal responsibility.

Before bringing up heavily charged material, such as in doing trauma work especially but, realistically, in *any* kind of case where the client's distress is substantial, you want to make sure the person has the resources to manage that emotional load. The client will need to have a vehicle for moving into and out of the feelings, typically employing a useful dissociation strategy in hypnosis to separate feelings from memories and past hurts from future predictions.

Tip #28 The greater the resistance, the greater the need for indirection.

Some approaches to hypnosis are entirely direct. The clinician knows what he or she wants the client to do, and without reservation tells the client in no uncertain terms just what that is. A direct approach deals directly with the presenting problem: the client comes in to stop smoking and the clinician talks about stopping smoking. Direct approaches also ask the client for the desired response directly: the clinician wants the client to sit down and so tells the client to sit down. For the approach to work, the client must be compliant. There's nothing subtle about direct approaches.

At the other end of the continuum are the indirect approaches which only indirectly deal with the presenting problem or desired response: instead of talking about smoking the clinician talks in detail about going sailing, enjoying the smell and taste of fresh air at sea and then asks rhetorically, "why would anyone want to breathe anything else?" Instead of telling the client to sit down, an indirect approach might lead one to ask, "Have you had the chance yet to find out how comfortable that chair is?"

Direct approaches are clear, but the client may also perceive them as threatening. Indirect approaches may be less threatening, but they are also more vague and may even seem evasive. Since both approaches have clinical merit in general, the salient clinical question concerns how to know whether to be more direct or indirect in your approach.

When hypnosis practitioners become enamored with the innovative work of the late psychiatrist, Milton Erickson, the first to develop indirection as a vehicle of treatment, they often mistakenly believe indirection is the best approach. Erickson was equally comfortable being direct and indirect, and varied his approach based on the client's characteristics, not how clever he was feeling that day. This is a good model to follow. If you only know how to be direct, there will be many reluctant, ambivalent, guarded, non-compliant people who will not respond well and you're now out of approaches. If you also know how to be indirect, then you can better reach people who won't feel pushed to comply and will respond in their own way and at their own pace.

Most people just don't like to be told what to do, even when the message is a good one. Thus, here is a general guideline: the greater the resistance, the greater the need for indirection. If you have a client who is responsive and is willing to comply with your directives, then you really don't need to be indirect.

Tip #29 Promote uncertainty to build responsiveness.

When people are quite certain about something, *anything*, it is incredibly difficult to change their minds. As family therapy pioneer Salvador Minuchin has often said, "Certainty is the enemy of change." Certainty when it works to your advantage or when you are right isn't usually the issue in the context of psychotherapy. To the contrary, it's when someone is absolutely certain and absolutely *wrong* that the problems surface.

Clients can come to therapy having terribly erroneous but firmly entrenched beliefs about themselves ("I'm a failure because I got a B on the exam"), about others ("No one *ever* tells the truth anymore") or about life itself ("Life is a burden to just be endured"). If you as the clinician directly contradict the client's belief, you will likely run smack into the walls that hold those ideas rigidly in place. Beliefs are self-stabilizing, and the mechanism that makes them so is called "cognitive dissonance." Cognitive dissonance is the inability to hold two contradictory views simultaneously. You can't simultaneously think of yourself as a good person and a bad person. If you believe you're a good person and I tell you I think you're not, will you change your view of yourself? No, you are far more likely to tell yourself that I'm clearly "having a bad day." Your view of yourself has stayed the same as you reject my contradictory feedback. If your self-image is a poor one and I tell you I think you're wonderful, will your view of yourself change? No, you are much more likely to conclude I'm saying this to manipulate you into satisfying some ulterior motive. As a clinician, when you provide positive feedback to a client who doesn't share your view, you can easily be dismissed as saying that "because clinicians get paid to say fake complimentary stuff like that."

Directly contradicting the client's viewpoint is not usually an effective intervention. Structuring a hypnosis session to gently ask rhetorical questions that lead the client to say, "I don't know" to themselves in reply, offering stories of people who were very sure but very wrong, and reminding the client of times in his or her life where it was necessary to adapt some perspective he or she once held to a change in circumstances. Milton Erickson viewed the typical cause of peoples' problems as "rigidity," and the way he applied hypnosis so creatively was to introduce *flexibility* in perceptions and behavior to his patients. Inducing uncertainty as a precursor to change was one of his best therapeutic tips for increasing responsiveness to his interventions.

Tip #30 Often, the people who most need the experience of hypnosis are the ones who are most afraid of it.

For too many people, their internal world is painfully toxic. It can become toxic through a crippling perfectionism, a debilitating self-doubt, a constant flooding of traumatic memories, a pervasive sense of emptiness, a bewildering barrage of painful emotions, a fear of vulnerability to the influence of Satan through hypnosis or other "scary mind stuff," or any of the other myriad of ways that define their inner world as a place to avoid at all costs. One of the many goals of any treatment, but especially treatment with hypnosis, is to empower the client.

Despite the mythology that hypnosis will disempower people, the opposite is true. As a clinical psychologist providing psychotherapy to individuals, couples and families, I was regularly tasked with how to help people become stronger and more resourceful. No one ever asked me to "help me lose control of myself." People always wanted *more* control, not less, and hypnosis helped in that worthy endeavor. But, not everyone wants to "go inside" and enjoy a peaceful or purposeful exploration of ways they can move forward in their life. If inside is a "bad place," people will evolve all kinds of mechanisms for avoiding going there.

In such cases, though, it is part of the solution to learn how to "go inside" and not automatically get lost in the toxicity. To go through life afraid of yourself, afraid of what's inside you, means you can never really relax or get comfortable within yourself. Instead, you must always find ways to occupy yourself and be anxiously hypervigilant about avoiding quiet moments of reflection. It's a treadmill you can't get off until you learn to go inside and find what's *right* with you instead of reflexively going straight to what's wrong with you.

Thus, if you suggest hypnosis and the person instantly dismisses the possibility, you need to take a closer look at why. If you begin hypnosis and the person bolts out of the experience just seconds into it because he or she instantly goes to something bad or painful, that doesn't mean you shouldn't do hypnosis. You don't want to reinforce the client's painfully limited view of him or herself. That's the person who most needs to learn how to go "inside" and find something positive instead of rigidly always going to the hurt. There may be hurt inside, but there are good things in there, too. Gentle guidance in small doses to help the person get comfortable with all the things inside that aren't bad is important to start the process of helping the client redefine him or herself in better and more expansive terms.

Tip #31 If the client has difficulty closing his or her eyes, then do the hypnosis session with his or her eyes open.

Relaxation is *not* the essential ingredient of successful hypnosis. In fact, there is a substantial research literature on "active-alert hypnosis" that highlights peoples' capacity to experience hypnosis and generate a wide variety of complex hypnotic phenomena (including dissociation and anesthesia) even when they are actively engaged in some strenuous or demanding activity.

When athletes are "in the zone" performing their sport, their eyes are open. When someone is absorbed in a good book or movie, his or her eyes are open. When someone is intensely focused on writing the exam, his or her eyes are open. When working with young children, their eyes are open when engaging them hypnotically through play, the medium in which they are most likely to become absorbed. Clearly, eye closure *isn't* an essential ingredient in doing hypnosis. It's helpful in general as a means to minimize outside distractions, but it isn't essential.

It helps to know this when you encounter those clients – and you will if you haven't already – who find eye closure threatening for any of a variety of reasons. For some people, they say it just "feels weird" to close your eyes and get internally focused when there's another person in the room. For some people, they say it makes them "feel vulnerable," as if by closing their eyes they are easier prey for the clinician's imaginary intrusions or manipulations. For some others, as mentioned above, closing their eyes and going inside instantly leads them right to the memories of abuse or trauma and they want to avoid that at all costs.

So, some of the most sensitive sessions a clinician can do may require him or her to conduct the hypnosis session with a client who has open eyes. It's imperative that you verbalize something that reinforces the client's need to feel in control such as, "You can keep your eyes open if you wish… or you can close them if you prefer… it's entirely up to you how you might *choose* to *get absorbed* in some of the new ideas and possibilities I'll be describing to you… that can really make a difference…as you focus and your comfort slowly grows." It's important to communicate acceptance of the client's choice and also reinforce that "there are many ways to learn" new skills and perspectives. Gradually, as such fragile clients get more experienced and comfortable with hypnosis, and begin to discover that there's more to their inner world than just the toxic or frightening, they can become and often are the clients who show some of the most dramatic improvements.

Tip #32 Avoid duplicating techniques that the client associates with failure.

If you or someone else has previously done hypnosis with this client and it didn't go well, in subsequent hypnosis sessions go out of your way to make sure you do something different. If you were the one who did the previous session that was less than successful, then you already know what approach you used with that client that you won't want to use again. Debriefing the client about what was and wasn't helpful from that session provides you with the feedback you need to expand on what was useful and develop another way to approach the design and delivery of the session to replace what wasn't helpful.

Both in theory and in practice, the clinician would have to have the attitude that adapting the session to the client's feedback is important to do, an attitude that is harder to actualize if you simply use scripted approaches. If you were not the one who did the previous session(s) that was deemed ineffective at least and negative at most, then debriefing the client is again an important thing to do to get as clear an idea as possible about what it was exactly that the client didn't like or find useful. Get as specific a description as you can about what the clinician did in terms of his or her techniques that the client associates with failure. The more specific a description you can get, the more easily you can choose another approach that will better fit the client based on what he or she says about the experience.

Thus, asking a client questions such as, "Do you recall how the hypnosis session began? Do you remember what it was about the approach he or she employed with you that wasn't helpful to you? Do you have any recollection about what sorts of things he or she said to you during the session that you found ineffective?" So, for example, when you find out the clinician used a countdown technique ("10....relax, 9...becoming more comfortable, 8... and so on) and the client says, "I hated it because I have a math phobia and numbers just freak me out!", you now know not to do a countdown induction or use mathematically based suggestions.

Generally speaking, if you take the time to ask the client what he or she is likely to find helpful, he or she will tell you, and you can include those preferences. What a difference to be client focused instead of technique focused!

Tip #33 Hypnosis is not a lie detector or a means to discover "the truth."

One of the persistent myths about hypnosis is that you can use it to excavate buried memories and thereby discover "what *really* happened." This issue has been studied extensively and it has become crystal clear that hypnosis can work in the *worst* of ways in regards to memory enhancement: the hypnotized person can recall more false details with a higher level of confidence. Thus, the person is very *wrong* and very *sure.*

This happens to be one of the principal reasons why the field of forensic hypnosis has nearly disappeared. It was a robust field years ago in which hundreds of American law enforcement agencies employed investigators who regularly used hypnosis to try to enhance eyewitness testimony and reduce crime related emotional traumas. Then, as the evidence became ever clearer that too many false details were derived from their forensic investigations, the courts became much more wary of hypnotically generated testimony.

Legal positions regarding hypnosis in the courts now range from *open admissibility* of material generated in hypnosis to a *per sé exclusion* where no testimony derived during hypnosis is admissible to a *rule with guidelines* where hypnotic testimony can be admitted *if* the investigation was conducted according to established investigation guidelines. Since each country has different laws and each state in the U.S. has its own legal position about hypnosis, it is a good idea for you to find out the position of the courts in the state or country where you live. It may make a big difference in how you conduct your sessions, especially those sessions involving age regression.

When someone asks you to do hypnosis to help him or her uncover memories to find "the truth" about what happened to them, your answer should be an emphatic "no." It is imperative to explain that hypnosis is *not* a lie detector and that the very act of digging for memories can unintentionally create them and make them indistinguishable from "real" memories.

Tip #34 Don't believe a memory is true just because it's detailed or emotional.

If you have ever seen a past-life regression or alien abduction hypnosis session, you can't help but notice how much vivid detail the people provide about their experiences. If you've never watched such sessions, visit *YouTube*. People can provide an amazing number of details that are plausible for the circumstances (the era or the spaceship), and they can provide them with a clarity and certainty that may seem compelling to the listener. They can also be highly emotional as they narrate their experience. Thus, the person who is an Egyptian slave building the pyramids in his or her regression or the person who is being subjected to invasive experiments by the extraterrestrials in his or her regression can cry, hyperventilate, scream, and experience *any* emotion intensely. It's clear that people can generate voluminous details and strong emotions for experiences that not only can't be verified but are *highly* unlikely. The people conducting these sessions should know how strong a role they play in generating these fantasy experiences rather than leading people to believe they're helping them uncover real experiences.

Let's take this a step further. When someone has detailed and emotional "memories" of having just been born and "clearly hearing" his or her mother admit that "this baby was an accident" as the basis for his or her "feeling unwanted all my life," can this really be a true memory? How exactly would a newborn understand mom's language? The client believes it to be true, acts as if it's true, bases his or her perceptions and emotional well being on it as if it's true. But, a newborn overhearing mom's confession and storing it as a memory to then be accurately recalled in some form decades later is… unlikely.

Clinicians tend to be empathetic and affirming people who are inclined to believe what their clients say. As stated earlier, though, hypnosis is *not* a lie detector. Without external evidence, there is no reliable way to distinguish a true memory from a confabulation. One of the ways, then, a clinician can do actual harm is conducting these kinds of sessions that serve to reinforce arbitrary beliefs in clients who are already lacking the ability to distinguish reality from fantasy. Using hypnosis to teach the all-important skill of "reality-testing" is especially important for people whose lack of critical thinking skills may drive their problems.

Tip #35 Affect can be dissociated, so beware of the "I've got a feeling" trap.

One of the most common and illustrative of the stage hypnotist's "tricks" is when he or she instructs the subjects to "imagine a screen on which you can watch the funniest movie you've ever seen." The subjects begin to slowly laugh and very soon they're laughing uproariously, holding their sides and trying to catch their breath. The audience loves it. Then the hypnotist will suggest, "Now the movie is turning sad, really sad." The subjects' laughter stops, and slowly turns to sobbing. Soon the sobbing gives way to crying and wailing. Next the hypnotist suggests, "Now the movie is turning funny again, very, very funny." And, on cue, the subjects all begin to laugh uproariously again.

All of this is interesting, of course, because it illustrates what is called the *induction of affect*, the generation of emotion through suggestions given in hypnosis. But the even more interesting thing is what happens next when the hypnotist goes from subject to subject asking the question, "What's so funny about your movie?" Can you predict the subjects' responses? Every one of them, or nearly every one of them, will reply, "I don't know."

What do you make of this display? It illustrates a point that is critical to good therapeutic practice. It shows us that affect can be dissociated. The subjects can have very strong feelings of funny or sad, but *they aren't tied to any specific context.*

Now consider the clinical implications in one of the more delicate scenarios clinicians who know hypnosis occasionally find themselves in. What happens when a client comes in and says, "I have the *feeling* I was abused, but I don't have any memories like that. Can you use hypnosis to help me find the memories?" Your answer 100% of the time should be an emphatic "no."

For clinicians who don't know about hypnosis or the potential for a dissociation of affect, they typically and dangerously assume that if there's a feeling, there must be some related causal situation to account for it. Now you know that's not true. You also know from previous discussions that the very act of digging for presumed memories can create them unintentionally. Beware the hazards when someone says, "I've got a feeling."

Tip #36 Make use of presuppositions to build expectancy.

A positive expectation for good results is a core component of successful treatments. Without a positive expectation that treatment can help, why would someone bother to go to a therapist or expend the effort to do the homework the therapist assigns? The research on the relationship between the quality of one's expectations and the quality of one's therapy outcomes makes it clear that positive expectancy is a driving force of successful therapies.

Consider what you as a clinician do to build positive expectations for your treatments. There are many ways of doing this, of course, but the point is it needs to be done. Despite that, therapists generally pay little attention to this important factor, much less make it a deliberate goal in the earliest stages of treatment. Given how important positive expectations are for seeking and participating in treatment, and how much they influence the rate and quality of treatment outcomes, building expectancy should be a primary goal in the very beginning of therapy. Hypnosis is an ideal vehicle for building expectancy in treatment. One such hypnosis strategy for building positive expectancy was described step-by-step in my book, *Treating Depression with Hypnosis: Integrating Cognitive-Behavioral and Strategic Approaches.*

Helping people develop the perception that well-targeted effort will yield benefits is vital. The pioneering strategic therapist, Paul Watzlawick, said it well when he said, "*It is the future, not the past, that determines the present; the prophecy of the event leads to the event of the prophecy.*"

The use of language that suggests positive future possibilities represents another way to establish "the prophecy of the event." When you employ a type of suggestion called a "presupposition," your suggestion presupposes the desired response. For example, suggesting that "*When* you find yourself responding differently in that situation..." presupposes this will happen. Suggesting that "*After* you get home you might be surprised by how much better you feel" presupposes what you will experience after you get home. Presuppositions represent a language of change, quietly promoting the belief that a change will happen *due to, because of, when*, some event, either internal or external, occurs.

PART 3

Tip #37 Expand the client's sensory experience during hypnosis.

Neuroscientific studies involving the use of brain scans (fMRI, PET, etc.) show how the use of sensory-based language activates the region of the brain associated with that sensory modality. Language that invites imagery activates the visual cortex, language that encourages the sense of smell activates the olfactory cortex, and so on.

If your suggestions don't specify a sensory modality, the probability is your client will respond with the sensory components of that experience that are usual for him or her. Thus, if you suggest taking a stroll through a beautiful garden, clients will likely focus on the sensory details of that experience that they associate with strolling through a garden. For one person, it might be the visual details of the different flowers, such as the size or color of the flowers. For someone else, it might be the fragrance of all the flowers or the warmth of the sun on his or her face that are the focal point. For someone else, it might be the feelings of enjoyment of being outside on a pretty day and feeling leisurely while strolling through the garden.

It's a general truth that nothing gets into your brain from the outside that doesn't pass through your senses first. But, not all senses are developed or relied upon equally. So, it helps to know something about how your client relates to an experience such as a stroll through a garden if that's the type of induction you intend to use. If such a stroll is always or nearly always represented in one primary modality, such as visual imagery, if you offer suggestions that amplify the visual details, you may be making it easier for the person to connect to the experience. However, if you continue to just focus on the visual details, you are now simply reinforcing what the client already knows how to do, namely visualize. What you can do is start to shift this person's focus to those other sensory components of the garden experience that he or she doesn't normally pay attention to. By bringing these into the experience, it broadens and deepens the experience and thus makes it that much more powerful and memorable.

Similarly, if you have an emotional client and you focus on the emotion, you're reinforcing the focus he or she already has that is part of his or her problem. What makes therapy work is *complementarity*: the goal is to *develop undeveloped or under-developed parts of the person* that are relevant to therapeutic progress. Mr. Spock doesn't need cognitive therapy – he fully grasps the merits of logic. Some emotion-focused therapy would be good for him, though…

Tip #38 People differ in the degree of amnesia they may experience following hypnosis.

Many people experience a "spontaneous amnesia" for the content of their hypnosis session. They emerge from the hypnosis session with little or no recall for what you talked about during the session. In contrast to a suggested amnesia, not often a desirable goal when you're trying to teach somebody something, a "spontaneous amnesia" was *not* suggested. It arose spontaneously, hence the name. The more profound the quality of dissociation the client experienced during the session, the greater the likelihood of developing amnesia for it.

One of the great hypnosis researchers, theorists and practitioners was psychologist Theodore X. "Ted" Barber. He postulated different personality types relative to the experience of hypnosis, one of which he termed the "amnesia-prone personality." This is the person who gets so absorbed internally so as to disconnect from the immediacy of the environment, including the clinician doing the hypnosis.

Perhaps surprisingly, even though the amnesia-prone client may not remember things you said during the session after re-orienting from hypnosis, your suggestions may "pop up" later and take effect. This phenomenon is what gave rise to the "trust your unconscious" position some advocate. But, more often than not, the amnesia simply leads to the suggestions being "lost in space." If your client doesn't remember much from the session, and nothing new and helpful emerges in-between sessions, then this indicates the need for you to make the hypnosis session more interactional. You can do this by asking for verbal interaction or, at least, finger signaling in response to your suggestions and questions. It's harder for your client to drift off and lose the thread of the session if you interact with him or her during hypnosis.

Amnesia-prone personalities aside, most clients will have *some* amnesia for the session, especially the middle part of the session. Learning theory and memory research describe the "primacy" and “recency” effects in which people are most likely to remember the first and last parts of a learning task or experience respectively. This describes well what often happens in hypnosis. The client will likely remember your induction and your suggestions for closure and reorientation, but only recall bits and pieces of what you talked about in the middle. Again, the more you engage clients during the session, the more of the session they will be likely to remember. Recording your sessions and giving the recording to the client certainly works against amnesia, but provides the therapeutically greater benefit of the repetition of ideas.

Tip #39 You can re-traumatize someone by revivifying a traumatic memory.

Working with clients who have suffered a history of trauma poses special challenges. On one hand, you provide *support* to the client while, on the other hand, you also provide a *challenge* to go beyond what happened and no longer be defined by it. Anyone who overcomes a history of trauma reaches a level of self-definition that is no longer rooted solely in the trauma. This is why the "you're more than your history" suggestion is so important to convey at the appropriate time in treatment.

Memory researchers make a distinction between what are termed "observer memories" and "field memories." An observer memory is one where you are not in the memory; rather you are an observer of some event(s) from a safe or comfortable distance. In hypnosis parlance, this is the form of regression called "hypermnesia" or a "dissociated regression." A field memory is one where you are directly connected to the event(s) emotionally and physically. You are *in* that memory. In the language of hypnosis, this is the form of regression called a "revivification." The client is reliving the memory as if that past event is going on *right now.*

The emotional intensity of a memory is partially determined by the way you go about remembering the episode. As you'd predict, revivification is the more emotionally impactful of the two approaches. The hypnosis research goes a step further on this subject: Having someone transition from an observer to a field memory during the course of the hypnosis session will *increase* the emotional intensity of the experience. Likewise, having someone transition from a field memory to an observer memory will *decrease* the emotional intensity of the experience.

If you jump right into a revivification process, the emotions can get quite intense, and not necessarily in a therapeutically helpful way. This can actually re-traumatize the client who is now subjectively back in the traumatic situation but still without any way to escape or without any new empowering resources with which to cope more effectively. Before revivifying a trauma, it's important to first establish an "escape hatch," a clear way the client can step out of the memory into a "safe place" if things get too intense or overwhelming.

Tip #40 Focusing each session on trauma or other deeply painful issues can be counterproductive.

Trauma has received a great deal of attention from the mental health profession, as it should. Clients come into therapy and tell horrific stories of unimaginable abuses and traumas they have experienced and the suffering they have endured. Therapists are a special breed of people, moved by human suffering and wanting to do something to help alleviate it. But, dealing skillfully with the pain in peoples' lives requires recognizing that there's a danger in getting too absorbed in or focused on someone's distress. Just as the research shows that focusing people on their anger ("pound this pillow and get your anger out") makes them angry, *not better,* repetitively focusing each session on emotional pain can amplify it and thereby make it even harder to help reduce its hold on the client.

Hypnosis can be a powerful tool in the treatment of trauma, and has been well integrated into a variety of treatment modalities. Clinicians routinely use hypnosis to help clients achieve such therapeutic objectives as:

- developing a goal (future) orientation rather than focusing only on the past;
- creating a solid support network;
- clarifying responsibility issues to reduce self-blame;
- clarifying control issues to reduce an ongoing sense of still being a victim of the past;
- establishing a comforting internal "safe place" to go to when distressed; and,
- developing critically important compartmentalization skills to clearly separate past influences from current choices and reactions.

With complex goals such as these, it would be easy to spend session after session focusing on the trauma and its consequences. However, a continued focus on trauma without providing some intermittent relief can itself become painful. If every time you do hypnosis your focus is on past hurts, then it shouldn't surprise you when your client says, "No!" when you say, "OK, let's do hypnosis now."

You work against yourself as well as the client when you don't mix sessions up with some emotionally heavy things as well as some lighter things. Soon the client doesn't want to do hypnosis any more simply because it's too painful. It's a good idea to let the emotional tone of sessions vary enough to keep the person engaged in the process.

Tip #41 Do your best to prevent the session from ending on a negative.

Dealing with the awful things that go on in peoples' lives means hypnosis sessions can be focused on painful memories, distressing symptoms, paralyzing fears, debilitating despair, crippling grief, and a surrender to hopelessness. Even during hypnosis sessions that are meant to provide relief, a client can easily end the session abruptly, opening his or her eyes and declaring that the session is over because "it's just too painful." Obviously, the clinician will have to respond to the client's distress in some manner that conveys both empathy and a plausible rationale for going forward together, albeit in a different way. It would be especially important to re-introduce hypnosis at this time but move it in the direction of something lighter or easier to speak to that can gradually yield a positive ending to the session.

Ending the session on a negative is undesirable. In general, whenever you can move the session in a positive direction, then strive to do so. This is especially important to do at the session's end. Here's why: The "recency effect" described earlier reveals how people are more likely to remember the most recent items or events they were exposed to.

In practical terms, this means the client will most likely associate hypnosis to those qualities that were present at the close of the session. If the hypnosis session ends badly, even if there were some good things that took place before things turned bad, the client is more likely to remember only the bad. Once the client has formed a negative association to hypnosis, he or she may become hesitant about or even unwilling to do hypnosis again.

Even if it means the session runs overtime, it will be to your advantage as the clinician as well as to the benefit of the client to encourage going right back into hypnosis (after debriefing the negative reaction) and doing something that will allow the session to end on a positive note.

People may not necessarily remember what you said, but they are *very* likely to remember how you made them feel.

Part 4:

Tips for Delivering Hypnosis Sessions

Tips for Delivering Hypnosis Sessions

Once the hypnosis session has begun, hopefully it engages the client's attention and absorbs him or her in the unfolding of the experience. The foundational concepts and tips for establishing a therapeutic framework and designing the session provided earlier can now come to fruition. This section provides tips for amplifying your therapeutic messages as you verbalize your suggestions. The words you say and the way you say them are your only tools, and anything that helps make those tools more effective can give rise to better therapeutic outcomes.

List of Tips for Delivering Hypnosis Sessions

Tip #42: Hypnosis *isn't* sleep. Don't use obsolete words or phrases associated with sleep in your hypnosis sessions.

Tip #43: Use a style that creates possibilities and promotes internalization.

Tip #44: Use a calm voice and demeanor that is consistent with encouraging relaxation and personal growth.

Tip #45: Challenges create power struggles with the client that you can't win.

Tip #46: "Trance logic" can be a blessing or a curse.

Tip #47: Give people the amount of time they need to respond.

Tip #48: People's degree of involvement in the hypnotic process will naturally fluctuate.

Tip #49: Build an increasing level of responsiveness as the session progresses.

Tip #50: Keep your attention on the client at all times during hypnosis.

Tip #51: Train yourself to observe without interpreting.

Tip #52: Check in with the client *during* the session to see if the session is on track.

Tip #53: Ask questions neutrally, without presuppositions, if you want a more accurate report from the client.

Tip #54: Always ask for permission before you touch someone.

Tip #55: Always do exactly what you say you're going to do.

Tip #56: Anything can be utilized, but be selective.

Tip #57: Anticipate likely distractions in your work environment and have suggestions prepared in advance for incorporating them into the process.

Tip #58: People can get emotional during hypnosis. Be prepared.

Tip #59: You don't have to stay with a technique or style if it isn't working.

Tip #60: Use adjectives that help amplify the desired response.

Tip #61: Use hypnosis to prepare the client to carry out homework assignments.

Tip #62: The best metaphors are generally the ones that come out of the client's direct experience.

Tip #63: Frame the metaphor then invite the client into the metaphor to make it more personal and prescriptive.

Tip #64: The more specific your post-hypnotic suggestions, the more effective they're likely to be.

Tip #65: Re-alerting is a gradual process.

Tip #66: Debrief sessions, if not right away, then at the next meeting.

Tip #42 Hypnosis *isn't* sleep. Don't use obsolete words or phrases associated with sleep in your hypnosis sessions.

The word "hypnosis" is derived from the name Hypnos, the Greek god of sleep. When the term hypnosis was coined in the 19th century, hypnosis was viewed as a special form of sleep, and sleep terminology was routinely embedded in hypnosis procedures. The view of hypnosis as a special form of sleep persisted well into the 20th century, until the young field of neuroscience became able to empirically measure brain activity.

Early EEG studies made it abundantly clear that hypnosis was *not* sleep and, in terms of neurological measures, in no way resembled sleep at all. Most hypnosis practitioners easily updated their language to exclude references to sleep during their hypnosis sessions, but there are still some practitioners who continue to use the archaic terminology (such as somnambulism, a diagnosable sleep disorder featuring sleepwalking, to characterize a deep state of hypnosis) and concepts equating hypnosis with sleep in their hypnosis procedures.

Since hypnosis is not sleep, any use of sleep-related terminology misrepresents the experience of hypnosis, which is never a good practice. Furthermore, by misrepresenting hypnosis in this way, it sets up unrealistic expectations on the part of the client, often giving rise to the client who deems his or her hypnotic experience a failure at its conclusion because "I heard everything you said." The client expected to be unconscious, oblivious to the suggestions being given, a misconception too easily developed when the practitioner encourages the client to "go deeper and deeper asleep" and closes the session with the command to "wake up at the count of three."

Besides the questionable style of such suggestions, they are simply misleading as to what goes on during hypnosis. The client is awake, focused, attentive, and thus fully capable of actively participating in the session, even determining which suggestions are relevant and worthy of consideration. If you want your clients to have a realistic expectation about the experience of hypnosis, then it's time to put the sleep terminology associated with an obsolete representation of hypnosis to bed.

Tip #43 Use a style that creates possibilities and promotes internalization.

Most people don't like to be told what to do even when it's for their own benefit. One of the key ways approaches to hypnosis differ from one another concerns the *style* in which suggestions are offered. The styles range from "authoritarian" at one end of the continuum to "permissive" at the other end.

An authoritarian style is imposing in nature. It tells people what to do ("You will open your eyes when I count to three") and encourages compliance as the ideal response from the client. Many clients *will* comply, doing as they were told to do. This may please the authoritarian clinician, but it may pose some problems for the client as well as the therapeutic alliance.

A permissive style *elicits* responses from within the client rather than imposing demands on the client. As a style for offering suggestions, it offers possibilities about what you *can* experience, what you *may* find absorbing, and what *might* be interesting. It's the language of possibility, and is respectful by then accepting and utilizing the choices the client makes in response. For example, if I say permissively, "You can close your eyes, if you wish," and the person keeps his or her eyes open, then I can accept that and utilize suggestions for developing new insights that are "eye opening."

There is a big difference between *compliance* and *internalization*. Therapeutically, we want the client to *internalize* the helpful perspectives we're encouraging. Consider the example of driving the speed limit: Some people will drive the speed limit only because they fear getting a ticket (compliance), while others will drive the speed limit because they genuinely believe that's the safest speed at which to drive (internalization). From the outside, both are driving the speed limit, but from the inside the motivations couldn't be more different nor could the feelings (driving anxiously about getting a speeding ticket versus calmly driving). What a difference between somebody doing something because they choose to rather than doing it because they're supposed to! You can't make people respond to your demands without violating their sense of free will and the cost might be how the client feels in the relationship. Furthermore, it's incongruous to tell someone you want them to be more independent so "do what I tell you to do."

What hypnosis does exceptionally well is create possibilities. The client is the only one who can actualize those possibilities. Since you can't make someone pay attention or make them relax or make them do an age regression, it's almost always best to phrase suggestions respectfully in terms of "you can" rather than "you will."

Tip #44 Use a calm voice and demeanor that is consistent with encouraging relaxation and personal growth.

While the words you say are crucial to the effectiveness of the hypnosis session, the way you say them also matters. If you're trying to encourage an experiential rather than a merely intellectual response, a primary reason for doing hypnosis, then your tone of voice and way you use your body can either enhance or distract from that objective. If you want to help the client relax, a typical component of hypnotic inductions, then modeling that relaxation in your voice helps communicate that possibility to the client. Slowing the rate of your delivery and speaking in a calmer and softer voice are the non-verbal components of the communication that add emphasis to your message.

Likewise, the way you sit is another aspect of nonverbal communication that can either enhance or distract from the hypnotic experience. As you begin your induction and your rate of speech slows and your voice grows softer and soothing, you can begin to model the quality of stillness (the inhibition of voluntary movement typical of hypnosis called "catalepsy"). When your gesturing diminishes and your body becomes still, it nonverbally invites the client's stillness and deeper absorption. You can deliberately grow quieter in your voice and body and thus invite a calmer, more focused response on the part of the client. Your demeanor is a vital component of the hypnotic interaction, so it helps when you model what's possible and desirable for your client.

I make a distinction between "*doing* hypnosis" and "*being* hypnotic." Someone can do hypnosis without really being hypnotic. Being hypnotic means embracing your role as the agent of change and deliberately using your voice and body to model the quiet absorption of hypnosis. It also means using language, even when not formally doing hypnosis, to encourage positive possibilities.

Tip #45 Challenges create power struggles with the client that you can't win.

Some people are happy to be told what to do and readily follow your directives. That can be a good thing when it's a *selective cooperation* on the part of your client because he or she is willing to defer to your greater clinical expertise. It can also be a not-so-good thing when it's simply compliance. If we want to encourage empowerment, it's paradoxical to suggest "I can empower you but only if you obey me."

Most people, however, generally don't like to be told what to do even when your suggestions are benevolent. Thus, when you push some clients to comply with some suggestion or demand, you may get some pushback. This is a response that has historically been termed "resistance" on the part of the client. Countless words have been written about recognizing and overcoming resistance in clients during hypnosis, and most of these have framed resistance as a characteristic of the client. That may well be in some instances, but there may also be something about the clinician's approach that instigates the client's pushback.

In more traditional approaches to hypnosis, for example, the clinician will make use of tests or challenges to which the client is expected to comply. The clinician may say, "Your eyes are tightly closed and cannot open… you cannot open your eyes… the harder you try to open your eyes the more tightly shut they become… now try and open your eyes." There will be some clients who respond to the implication embedded in the suggestion that distinguishes "trying" from "doing" ("The harder you *try* to open your eyes the more tightly shut they become") and won't open their eyes. Other clients, though, assert their control to such suggestions by immediately opening their eyes. You challenged them to discover they couldn't open their eyes, but they "won" the challenge by defeating your suggestions. It's hard to recover your credibility when you suggested the client wouldn't be able to open his or her eyes and then he or she promptly did so. Blaming the client for being "resistant" isn't a solution.

This is the problem with including challenges and tests in clinical procedures. Any time you challenge a client to respond to some suggestion, whether for eye closure, an inability to bend or move an arm (called an "arm catalepsy"), remember some suggestion, hallucinate something, or whatever, you run the substantial risk of losing that challenge. My clients can defeat me 100 percent of the time by doing *nothing*. I'm not tough to beat, and neither are *you*. Thus, it's best to avoid making tests or challenges a part of your practice. Most of the time, challenges just lead to *power struggles* you are unlikely to win.

Tip #46 "Trance logic" can be a blessing or a curse.

The late psychiatrist and preeminent hypnosis researcher Martin Orne, M.D., occasionally did demonstrations of hypnosis that highlighted the non-rational nature of the experience of hypnosis. He would have his demonstration subjects sit with both hands resting on their thighs, then perform an arm levitation so that one arm was now floating in the air. Next he'd suggest that they look down and still see both hands resting on their thighs. When he then asked them to count their hands, they would look at one hand on one thigh and count "1," then see the other hand on the other thigh and count "2," and then see the hand floating in the air and count "3!" When Orne would look surprised and ask, "You have three hands?" research subjects would typically look mildly confused but say "yes." They looked mildly confused, but not upset or agitated.

Orne did this kind of demonstration in a number of different ways, always guiding the subjects to form perceptions of experiences that were objectively impossible.

He termed the ability to have such perceptions in hypnosis "trance logic."

Trance logic allows people to have experiences that may not be objectively possible, yet can still be meaningful. That's when trance logic is a blessing. For example, a creative clinician can encourage someone to have that "last goodbye" with a vividly imagined representation of someone who passed away, allowing him or her to say during hypnosis what he or she never had the chance to say before. This experience can afford the client a new and therapeutic sense of closure. The most creative things that happen in hypnosis are often due to the benefits of trance logic.

On the other hand, the fact that people can get so wrapped up in an experience that has no rational or objective basis means that a clinician who is inclined to use hypnosis in esoteric ways can get powerful reactions from people. Trance logic is, in part, what fuels past-life regressions, alien abduction regressions, rebirthing processes, and other esoteric uses of hypnosis. Trance logic can become a problem when clients get absorbed in arbitrary ideas that support magical or distorted thinking and thereby reduce the client's ability to think clearly about his or her experiences. This can lead to poor decisions and ineffective actions as well as a diminished sense of personal responsibility for the consequences of those decisions and actions.

In general, though, trance logic gives clinicians the chance to offer suggestions for things that can be clinically useful but make no objective sense. In fact, in the first demonstration of clinical hypnosis I ever saw, a woman with chronic leg pain was given the suggestion that her pain would turn to liquid and run down her leg and out onto the floor where it would be a "harmless puddle of pain." It worked! She found the imagery compelling and it provided her pain relief. A "puddle of pain" on the floor doesn't make logical sense, but to the person in hypnosis, it makes perfect sense through the mechanism of trance logic.

Tip #47 Give people the amount of time they need to respond.

Consider for a moment how long it generally takes you to "get into" whatever you're doing. If you exercise, it usually takes a little while before you fully get into your workout. If you're watching a movie, it usually takes a little while before you get into the characters and storyline. If you are taking an exam, it usually takes a little while before you develop the greater concentration it takes to do your best. There are countless experiences you have that you respond to by *gradually* getting into the "mindset" needed to maximize that experience. Hypnosis is that kind of experience for most people.

Hypnotic responses aren't usually formed rapidly. Rather, they take time to evolve. How much time they take will naturally vary from client to client. Generally, only the statistically uncommon so-called "high hypnotizables" (what hypnosis researcher Ernest Hilgard called the "hypnotic virtuosos") can generate complex hypnotic phenomena quickly. Since hypnosis is a multi-dimensional experience, not just an idea, it is important to an effective clinical practice to acknowledge and respect each client's personal pace for responding.

If you want people to generate multi-dimensional and fully experiential responses rather than merely intellectual ones, then giving people time to develop those responses is extremely important. Being observant throughout the hypnosis session as to how the client is responding is a good practice, and so is giving people a chance to be an active participant in the process. For example, you can suggest that, "when you're ready to go on to the next phase you can signal me by raising an index finger" (a suggestion for a nonverbal reply called an "ideomotor signal") as a means of checking in regarding the client's readiness for the next step in the process, whatever that step might be. This is one easy way to adapt to the client's experiential pace rather than expecting or requiring the client to adapt to yours.

Those who strive for "instant hypnosis" or "instant deepeners" or "instant *anything*" may get the client to *comply* with their push for some rapid, dramatic response, but there is too little chance for instant *internalization.* Such techniques may be good for the self-aggrandizement of the practitioner, but aren't methods that are respectful of the client and his or her individual pace of responding. There are no prizes for speed. That said, however, there are extreme contexts, such as an emergency room or the scene of an accident, where using abrupt authoritarian suggestions may help defocus from the ongoing trauma. But, in general practice, the goal isn't fast hypnosis. The goal is facilitating a meaningful hypnotic experience with a good therapeutic outcome.

Tip #48 People's degree of involvement in the hypnotic process will naturally fluctuate.

When people are absorbed in the experience of hypnosis, their attention narrows to whatever they're focused upon. As focused as someone might be, however, it does not preclude other thoughts, memories, sensations, and experiences from entering his or her awareness. Can someone be deeply absorbed in hypnosis and suddenly have the thought, "Oh, I forgot to pay my electric bill!"? Yes, someone can be engaged in the process and still have things come up that are utterly irrelevant to what's going on in the session. Typically, whatever that distraction might be is momentary and then the client's attention returns to what really matters. The point is that attention can and does wander during the hypnosis session and this is normal, to be expected and to be accepted as part of the process.

To suggest to a client that he or she "go deeper, deeper, deeper" into hypnosis is a suggestion that doesn't really parallel very well the actual experience of hypnosis. People's degree of involvement in the experience will naturally fluctuate. Hopefully, the client *will* become more deeply immersed in the experience as the session progresses. However, at any given moment, you might be saying "deeper, deeper" when, in fact, the person's experience is "lighter, lighter" because he or she just thought of someone he or she needs to call after the session is over, his or her stomach just rumbled, or some other distraction is diverting his or her attention. It's more realistic to suggest something along the lines of, "and as you gradually become more deeply absorbed in the possibilities… occasionally your mind will naturally wander… which is to be expected… because awareness naturally drifts from one thing to another… and each time you bring your focus back to my words… and your internal experience… it can deepen your comfort even further …"

Tip #49 Build an increasing level of responsiveness as the session progresses.

Hypnosis is an experiential process that typically encourages responses on many levels of experience concurrently. The majority of clients' responses are likely to be gradual. The hypnosis session's structure accounts for this by slowly leading the client in the direction of greater absorption in the process and increased responsiveness to suggestions as the session unfolds. The things you talk about, the suggestions you offer, are likely to be inherently of interest to the client since you are addressing his or her personal concerns. The client in hypnosis is usually attentive as he or she strives to find solutions to his or her problems in your words. But, attentive doesn't necessarily mean *responsive* if your suggestions don't fit for what could be any of a number of reasons, ranging from the suggestions missing the target to the person not wanting to hear an inconvenient truth. Thus, attentiveness is a start, but building responsiveness is key to generating hypnotic phenomena and therapeutic associations.

The primary means for building responsiveness from the beginning of the session is the establishment of a "response set." A response set is a tendency to respond in a particular way. The most commonly employed response set is called a "yes set," a tendency to respond in the affirmative. Pioneered by the late psychiatrist Milton H. Erickson, M.D., a yes set typically involves offering the client a series of statements called "truisms." Truisms are statements that are so obviously true there is no legitimate basis for disagreeing with them, such as, "Each person is unique"; "Sometimes life can be difficult"; and "Human beings can be complicated at times."

You naturally agree with each statement, silently saying "yes" to each one in your thoughts. When you say yes to the first statement, then yes to the second and third statements, what is your most likely response to the next statement? Yes, indeed! The yes set builds a momentum for the client generating likely yes responses to your further suggestions. So, all through the hypnosis session, you can offer ideas and feedback that the client can easily agree with, thereby increasing his or her willingness to respond agreeably to new possibilities as you go along.

Tip #50 Keep your attention on the client at all times during hypnosis.

When people are processing information, as in responding to suggestions during hypnosis, they inevitably manifest observable changes in physiology that can range from subtle to obvious. These manifestations include changes in muscular tension in the face and body, changes in the rate and quality of breathing, coloration changes in the face as it reddens or blanches, eye movements, changes in facial expression, and so on. In the language of hypnosis, these are termed "ideomotor responses," defined as automatic or non-volitional physical manifestations of mental experience.

An everyday example of an ideomotor response is when you're driving and you catch yourself tensely gripping the steering wheel of your car while you've been thinking of what a tough day you had at work. Your white-knuckle grip is the manifestation of the muscular tension associated with mentally reviewing the episodes that occurred during a difficult day. The fact that these ideomotor responses can be readily observed in people as they respond to your suggestions during hypnosis is the reason why focusing on your client throughout the session is so important.

Your client's observable ideomotor responses offer you an important source of information about what he or she is experiencing. But, if you don't observe those responses then you can't either inquire about them or utilize them as responses that can further generate other responses that might be helpful. There are some clinicians who learned, unfortunately, that it's okay or even desirable to go into hypnosis as they do hypnosis with their clients. So, they close their eyes as they conduct their hypnosis sessions, thereby cutting themselves off from their clients and their clients' nonverbal responses. That's a poor practice if you want to know anything about how your client is faring during the session. Thus, I encourage every clinician to stay attentive to his or her client's experience while conducting hypnosis sessions.

Tip #51 Train yourself to observe without interpreting.

Once you observe some change taking place in your client's appearance or behavior, such as a smile, grimace or flicker of tension across his or her face, it is a natural tendency to reflexively attach some interpretation to it. However, this is a reflex that needs to be resisted. The client's experience is ambiguous, and your projections or interpretations about what that smile, grimace or flicker of tension "means" may be way off from what your client is actually experiencing.

It requires a bit of humility to acknowledge that you're an outside observer and only your client can ever really know what he or she is experiencing inside. And, despite the client having a much better chance of knowing what's going on in terms of his or her subjective experience, it is quite common that sometimes even the client doesn't know: you ask what he or she thinks or feels about something or what he or she is experiencing and the answer is, "I don't know." It's potentially hazardous to assume you know more about the client's subjective experience than he or she does.

Furthermore, the way you are inclined to interpret the meaning of client responses is based on your beliefs and whatever model(s) of treatment you subscribe to, further increasing the likelihood that your interpretations will be at least somewhat distant from your client's views of what's going on. Here's a relevant example: Suppose you're conducting a hypnosis session with a client and the content of the session isn't particularly emotionally charged. The client is relaxed and focused, and seems to be doing just fine. Then, you observe a big, fat teardrop roll out of the client's eye. Do you assume the client is upset about something? If you inquire about his or her experience and are assured everything is fine, then what does it mean? Is it evidence of suppressed upset feelings? Or is it something else?

Before you assume the tear has some deep, psychological meaning, it's far more likely to just be lacrimation, a tearing of the eyes as the person relaxes. Tears clean the eyes and keep the eyes moist, and so can have an entirely neutral purely physiological function. But, if you ask a question with a presupposition embedded within, called a "leading question," such as "What are you upset about?" when you see a teardrop, the client can respond to the implication of the question. The client wasn't upset until *you* suggested he or she was upset. Now that you've suggested being upset, it's no surprise when the client becomes upset. Learning how to observe without interpreting can prevent many complications from arising during hypnosis sessions.

Tip #52 Check in with the client *during* the session to see if the session is on track.

During hypnosis, people can drift off into deeply dissociative experiences and lose the thread of the session's intent. People can also easily misinterpret things you say and form impressions quite distant from what you actually had in mind. No matter how sensitive or perceptive you might be, you're not a mind reader. If you want to know whether your client is deriving anything of value from your hypnosis session, there is only one way to find out: ask him or her directly for feedback. I'd recommend doing this *at least* once *during* the session.

If you're only going to check in once, then an ideal time to do so is towards the end of the session before you begin the wrap-up. By checking in, you can find out what the client heard (or didn't) and what it means to him or her. If the person got the point, you can reinforce the value of the point. But, if the person *didn't* get the point, you now have the opportunity to correct any misconceptions or misinterpretations that may be necessary to correct. If you wait until the session is over to debrief, then it is already too late to make corrections or adjustments unless you're willing and able to start another hypnosis session right away.

The process of checking involves three steps:

1. First letting the client know you intend to check in on his or her experience ("in just a moment I'd like to check in with you to find out what you're aware of right now");

2. Providing suggestions for facilitating his or her verbalizing easily what's going on ("and you'll be able to describe your experience out loud quite easily); and,

3. Using the verbalizations as a deepener ("and with each word that you say you can get even more deeply absorbed in the experience"). The client shares some of what he or she is experiencing, you get to

ask questions for clarification, and then you know much more of what's going on with the client. The check in can save you and your client a lot of trouble by getting things back on track before they go too far astray.

There are clinicians who have been doing hypnosis for decades who have never even once talked to the client during the hypnosis session. They have the unrealistic fear that talking during the session will somehow interfere with the quality or depth of the hypnosis experience. On the contrary, the check-in can dramatically alter the course of a session by making the hypnotic experience increasingly personal and meaningful.

Tip #53 Ask questions neutrally, without presuppositions, if you want a more accurate report from the client.

There is a phenomenon called "interrogatory suggestibility" that becomes evident when someone responds to the suggestions embedded within a question. When a question contains a presupposition, the client may respond to the presupposition without realizing that the quality of his or her response was influenced by that presupposition. For example, if you ask a client, "How angry were you?" it *presupposes* the emotion of anger was present and you're now requesting an assessment of the degree of that anger. Such questions are known as "leading questions," and the fact of their potential influence on the answer you receive requires that you give them extra consideration.

Elizabeth Loftus is a psychologist and memory expert who has studied leading questions extensively. She can show research subjects a video of a car accident and get quite different reports about what happened based on whether she asks the neutral question, "Did you see a STOP sign?" or asks the leading question, "Did you see the STOP sign?" The former asks if you saw *a* stop sign, questioning if one was there. The latter question suggests there was, indeed, a stop sign (*the* stop sign) and asks if you saw it. Asked as a leading question, many more people confidently reported seeing a STOP sign that wasn't actually there.

The potential for suggestions to alter memory, and even create entirely fictitious memories, is well established at this point. Thus, how you phrase questions during hypnosis can make quite a difference in what comes up for someone during the session. A leading question such as, "How were you abused?" posed to someone who never reported a history of abuse can have a devastating impact if he or she accepts the presupposition in the question. On the other hand, a leading question such as, "How happily surprised will you be when you notice your symptoms subsiding this week?" can have a wonderfully positive impact if the person absorbs the presupposition embedded in the question.

Therefore, it is important to master the skill of asking questions neutrally during hypnosis when you do the "check in" with the client. Asking the client, "Can you describe what you're aware of right now?" is neutral: it's not asking for a cognitive, emotional or physical appraisal specifically. Rather, it's asking what the client is aware of, and the client is free to answer in any way he or she pleases. If you want a less biased answer to your questions, it's generally a good idea to give the client the room to share whatever he or she wishes to share without being directed by the clinician whenever possible.

Tip #54 Always ask for permission before you touch someone.

Touching someone is an intimate gesture. It is an intrusion into personal space. This can be a welcome intrusion because it was invited, or it can be an unwelcome intrusion because it wasn't invited and was both unexpected and unwanted. Some practitioners of hypnosis have no apparent hesitation about touching people simply because they want to or because they're using some technique that requires it. I see this as disrespectful, invasive and even intimidating. With hypnosis as an amplifier of sorts, the issue of whether to touch the client becomes even more delicate.

Most of the time when you're conducting hypnosis sessions there is no need to touch the client. However, there are some occasions when touching the client is desirable or necessary. When you're conducting hypnosis sessions for the purpose of pain relief, touching the client in order to affirm and guide the development of hypnotic anesthesia is an invaluable and usually necessary part of the process. When you're helping someone deal with trauma, and especially when emotions are running hot and heavy, it can be a wonderfully kind and supportive gesture to hold a client's hand. A welcomed touch can be therapeutic, but an unwelcome touch can be a threat to the client and generate strong negative reactions. Thus, it is imperative to ask the client for permission to touch him or her before ever doing so.

Ideally you ask for permission twice, once *before* the session begins if you know touch will be a part of the process, and once at the time *during* the session when you would like to touch the client. If you're going to ask for permission only once, then during the session is usually the best time to ask. You can employ a suggestion such as, "In just a moment, I'd like to reach over and touch you on the back of your left hand. If that's alright with you, please signal me by raising the index finger of your right hand or verbally saying okay." When the person signals you (with an "ideomotor signal") or says okay, you have now been given permission to touch him or her and can then proceed with whatever you're going to do next. This is a respectful way of approaching the use of touch, and it again defines the client as the empowered one who holds the right to say yes or no.

Tip #55 Always do exactly what you say you're going to do.

Every therapeutic modality emphasizes the importance of the relationship between clinician and client. The "therapeutic alliance" encompasses many different factors, but none are more important than the level of trust the client has in the clinician. Trust can be damaged in many different ways, but one of the most common ways is when the clinician says one thing but does another in or out of hypnosis.

During the hypnosis session, though, when the client is particularly connected to the clinician and attentive to the clinician's words, if the words don't match the actions the incongruity stands out as if in dazzling neon. So, if you say you're "going to be silent for a minute of clock time while you focus on that new possibility," then be silent for a minute just as you said you would, not two or three minutes. If you say you're going to, with permission, touch the client "on the back of your left hand," then only touch the client on the back of his or her left hand. (It helps not to confuse right and left when you're sitting opposite someone!) Consistently doing what you said you would do is how the client comes to know that when you say something, you mean it, inspiring his or her trust in your integrity.

Tip #56 Anything can be utilized, but be selective.

One of Milton Erickson's many contributions to the fields of hypnosis and psychotherapy was his principle of utilization. Utilization in hypnosis means "utilizing" the client's experience as the basis for the various stages of hypnotic interaction.

Utilizing the client's previous experiences with hypnosis can be the basis for the induction when you suggest something such as, "Since you have had experience before with getting focused and relaxed… you can recall how good that experience felt… as you begin to experience again those good feelings now…" Utilization means using the client's beliefs, experiences, values, history, expectations, relationships, and responses as the basis for building new experiences.

Utilization also means using things going on during the hypnosis session itself, such as incorporating the routine sounds of the environment into the process when they arise, utilizing the client's reactions, and even utilizing the client's posture or physicality. To suggest, "As you continue to breathe deeply… as you are right now… each breath can allow you to get even more absorbed in comfort…" In this example, you're utilizing the client's breath as the deepener.

You can comment on someone's breathing, posture, facial expressions, movements, and so on, but to do so may actually serve to make the client self-conscious and thereby work against the larger aims of the session. Or, if you keep commenting on the sounds of the environment, you can easily lead someone to focus externally instead of internally and thereby miss making important therapeutic connections. So, the clinician has to be selective about what's worth commenting on and utilizing. You can utilize *anything*, but you certainly don't want to utilize *everything*.

Tip #57 Anticipate likely distractions in your work environment and have suggestions prepared in advance for incorporating them into the process.

No environment is perfect for doing hypnosis. Wherever you work, there are likely to be environmental intrusions, such as phones that ring in the middle of a session, low flying airplanes that rattle the windows, relentlessly barking dogs, announcements over the intercom, colleagues that stick their heads in and then apologize ("Sorry, I didn't know you were with someone") as they sheepishly retreat, traffic noise, safety vehicles with sirens blaring, and on and on.

Take a moment and think about the environment in which you do hypnosis and the different distractions that sometimes arise in that environment. You can't predict the exact moment that a familiar distraction will arise, but you know that it will sooner or later. You can be ready for it! Without missing a beat in your ongoing delivery of the hypnosis session, you can incorporate and utilize the distraction.

It would be a good use of forethought to list the distractions and then generate three or four really good suggestions that reframe those distractions as helpful by putting them in a positive and useful light. When the phone rings smack in the middle of a session, instead of saying "Darn it!", it might be better to say, "Isn't it comforting to know the phone can ring and there's nothing you need to do… so you can let each ring remind you… that you have the time and space here and now to be so deeply comfortable…"

When you take the time to generate positive frames for utilizing what might otherwise be distracting, you can easily memorize these and have them ready to go when a potential distraction arises. Being ready with statements that help keep the session on track can make all the difference between a focused and unfocused session.

Tip #58 People can get emotional during hypnosis. Be prepared.

When you're conducting hypnosis sessions, people often react in unexpected ways. Sometimes, people will become quite emotional during a session, and sometimes it's puzzling to the clinician because the reaction seemed to come out of nowhere. In more traditional circles this phenomenon is called an "abreaction."

An abreaction is when someone reacts in unexpected and emotional ways with unresolved issues and feelings that can spontaneously emerge with surprising intensity. Personally, I find the term abreaction an unnecessarily pathologizing label and prefer to simply acknowledge that people can get emotional during hypnosis sessions. Realistically, it really shouldn't be much of a surprise when people in therapy have the time and space to focus on their lives and things that happened that affected them and pent-up feelings emerge.

When they do, there's an opportunity to do some real healing work, a chance to get some resolution on some issue that has been simmering for some time. Offering emotional support to the distressed client is imperative, of course, but so is providing some direction towards resolution. Support without direction doesn't help the client develop new perspectives or better coping skills.

There are times when the clinician could not possibly have known some aspect of the client's history that gave rise to a strong reaction. However, there are other times the clinician can both anticipate and even prevent such reactions. Consider the client who has a significant history of trauma for whom the clinician begins a common "safe place" induction: "Sometime in your life… you've had the experience of being someplace where you felt safe… and you can go to that place in your mind *now*…" In response, the client starts the search for a safe place, but soon bursts into tears because he or she couldn't find one. Given the history of trauma, the client has *never* felt safe *anywhere.* This could have been anticipated and prevented by the thoughtful clinician who added the phrase, "...or you can *imagine* and *create* such a place..."

Prevention opportunities such as this are readily available to utilize throughout the session. This is especially true when your suggestions are phrased permissively and you present multiple options to the client who is encouraged and helped to choose wisely among them. Negative reactions are far more likely to occur when the clinician assumes an authoritarian position and is demanding of a response the client feels either unable or unwilling to provide.

Tip #59 You don't have to stay with a technique or style if it isn't working.

While it's true some people respond more slowly to hypnosis procedures than others, it's also true that some people just aren't going to respond to a particular approach for a variety of reasons: perhaps the approach is too esoteric, too authoritarian, too vague, too demanding, too demeaning, too fast or slow, or just too *something* the person is unable or unwilling to respond to. If you begin with some technique and the client just isn't responding well, should you stay the course and continue with that technique in the hope that eventually the client will respond? Probably not. As a general principle in doing hypnosis (and in life, too), if what you're doing isn't working, it's a good time to consider doing something else.

Before switching approaches, the first thing to consider is the client's "experiential pace," his or her personal pace for developing a useful focus. Some people take longer than others to get absorbed, of course, so you don't want to switch prematurely. But, if it doesn't seem to be a pacing issue, and the person just isn't getting into your approach, then what?

Doing more of what isn't working is unlikely to "win over" the client and generate a positive response. This can too easily become the basis for an entirely unnecessary power struggle. It's perfectly fine to check in with the client and get a report about what isn't working for him or her, and then use the feedback to offer him or her another approach. An attitude of curiosity on the part of the clinician makes it easier to transition to another approach as you wonder what a change in style might accomplish.

So, if you're halfway through a countdown induction, for example, you don't have to finish counting when it's clear to you that saying more numbers won't help this person engage with you. It's absolutely okay to switch mid-stream to another approach but take care not to do so too abruptly. Rather, you can make a statement or two that encourages an easy transition, such as, "I can continue to count...and you can continue to count...but what really counts... is discovering how much easier it can be for you to get comfortably absorbed... when I remind you that here's an opportunity... for you to discover... something important... worth focusing your attention upon..."

The transition is an easy one to make and opens up the possibility of getting absorbed in a way that's different from the vehicle of a countdown that didn't inspire much. The transition to another approach models the very essence of what therapy is all about: flexibility in adapting by doing something different when what you've been doing isn't working.

Tip #60 Use adjectives that help amplify the desired response.

When you're conducting hypnosis sessions, there is a goal you have in mind. The client usually makes it quite clear during the interview what the problem is and what he or she hopes therapy will accomplish. The task of the clinician, then, is to build the bridge *experientially* through hypnosis that helps the client get from "here" to "there." During the session, therefore, the clinician will be offering many suggestions about possible perspectives to hold and possible behaviors to engage in as the vehicle for the client getting where he or she wants to go. When you offer suggestions about possible feelings, attitudes, ideas, and behaviors to the client that are embedded in some larger therapeutic strategy, it's important to give these some extra power and potential impact by using adjectives that amplify them. Here are some examples:

- More than just the suggestion to find a memory to recall, "you can find a *happy* memory that you can *enjoy* recalling in *vivid* detail"
- More than just the suggestion to realize something, "you can develop an *empowering* realization that can make it easier to *courageously* take action"
- More than just the suggestion to have a new idea, "you can have an "*inspiring* idea that *energizes* you to *assertively* take charge of the situation in *bold* ways"

One of the many strengths of hypnosis is evident in the *induction of affect*, the suggested emotional associations that can help drive new thoughts, feelings, and behaviors in the direction of problem solving. You can deliberately use emotionally charged terms that are paired with words and phrases that encourage meaningful understandings and actions on the part of the client. Doing so can move therapy along at a more rapid rate and with a better quality of therapeutic outcomes.

Tip #61 Use hypnosis to prepare the client to carry out homework assignments.

Realistically, when so much of therapy involves education and specific skill building, there needs to be some vehicle for helping clients acquire the education and skills they need and then use them in their everyday lives. Homework assignments are a primary vehicle for promoting the acquisition and integration of new perspectives and skills beyond the therapy office.

There is a large body of research evidence that makes it clear that clients have a faster rate and better quality of result when therapies include the use of structured homework. There are many different types of homework assignments such as role plays, symptom prescriptions, ambiguous function tasks, skill building tasks, and externalization strategies, to name a few. The challenges to the clinician are about knowing what to assign and when, taking care to make sure the assignment is safe, relevant, acceptable, and instructive for the client. But, when clients aren't inclined to be proactive in their own behalf, even waiting passively for you to "fix" them, getting the client to carry out homework assignments can be difficult.

Negative expectations that inspire a "why bother?" attitude can easily preclude a willingness to do the assignment, so a positive expectancy is important. But, passivity can arise for other reasons as well, highlighting the value of addressing the issue of homework during the hypnosis session. Strategic and family therapy pioneer Jay Haley called this process of introducing the homework assignment during the hypnosis session "seeding." By orienting the client to the necessity of doing things differently in order to get better outcomes and using illustrative metaphors to that effect, the clinician can "plant the seed" that frames *action as desirable and likely to produce positive results.* This is a powerful means for motivating client action. The clinician can think in these terms: Where can I send the client and what can I ask him or her to do that will help him or her acquire the perspective and skills to help catalyze therapeutic progress?

The literature of strategic, action-oriented therapies contains a treasure trove of creative and helpful homework assignments. My books *Breaking the Patterns of Depression* and *Depression is Contagious* contain many dozens of homework assignments specific to treating depression and related issues. These can be useful in helping clinicians generate relevant homework assignments that can teach specific skills (such as coping, problem solving and social skills) to clients needing help developing such skills. During hypnosis the client is oriented to the aims of the skill and the benefits of acquiring it, and then after the hypnosis session ends the clinician can assign the skill-building task.

Tip #62 The best metaphors are generally the ones that come out of the client's direct experience.

In the practice of clinical hypnosis, metaphors have come to mean stories that you tell the client. Metaphors can have many different purposes, including diagnosis, building rapport, reframing meanings, and embedding solutions. There are many excellent books that are filled with wonderful stories that can be told to help a client get "unstuck" and see things from a different perspective. As valuable as these books containing metaphors are, they are stories about someone else in some other place under some other circumstances. Will the client be able to relate meaningfully to such stories?

When you tell stories about other people in other circumstances, it's vitally important that you encourage the client's *search for relevance*, the deeper consideration of how that story is related to his or her circumstances and what it might suggest that could be helpful. The search for relevance requires the client to actively engage with the story and make it personally meaningful.

The search for relevance is the driving force that makes metaphor a potentially powerful therapeutic tool. When someone listens to a story but doesn't either look for or see personal relevance, he or she might find the story entertaining, but not at all instructive.

However, when you tell a story to the client that is derived from a story that he or she told you during the interview or in earlier discussions, there is an immediate relevance that is missing when you're talking about someone else's experience. For example, when a client just happens to mention in passing that he worked his way through college as a waiter, it provides a basis for making the therapeutic point in hypnosis that hard work in the present in support of a greater goal can create new opportunities in the future. The client's own experience verifies that point. Likewise, when a client just happens to mention in passing that she started her own successful company on a shoestring budget, it provides a basis for making the therapeutic point in hypnosis that a willingness to take sensible risks can yield big results.

By using the client's stories, experiences directly taken from his or her personal history, and giving them a therapeutic frame, there is a personal connection that is far more powerful than telling stories of old Greek myths or little bunny rabbits. These can be effective, too, of course. But the larger point here is that each person's personal history naturally matters more to him or her than does anyone else's, so it's a good idea to use it when you can.

Tip #63 Frame the metaphor then invite the client into the metaphor to make it more personal and prescriptive.

Metaphor is by its very nature an indirect style of communication. After all, the story is often about someone else in some different time and place. This represents one of the many paradoxes to be found in the application of hypnosis: *this story isn't about you... but this story is about you.*

Since the story may be about someone else in some other circumstance, particularly when you have a guarded or ambivalent client (the greater the resistance the greater the need for indirection), there is an implicit suggestion that the reason the story is being told is because it has relevance to the client. Will the client engage in the search for relevance and thereby strive to uncover some personal meaning in the story as the clinician intends? Maybe... but maybe not. Depending on how far removed the story is from the client's circumstances, how proactive the client is or isn't in looking for meaning in life experiences in general, and whether the clinician encourages an active search for relevance, some clients may sit back and simply enjoy the story and completely miss its therapeutic messages.

The technique of "framing the metaphor" is a vehicle for introducing the story as having some potential value to the client: "I'd like to tell you about a man I met years ago that said something once I've never forgotten that might have some meaning to you as well..." The technique of "inviting the client into the metaphor" is a means for encouraging the client to actively engage with the story, requiring the client to actively imagine being in the story's circumstances and consider how he or she might have reacted: "As I describe the situation this man in the story suddenly found himself in, I wonder what you would have done in that same circumstance... and what he did was the following..." This kind of imaginative involvement makes the story more interesting, more relevant, and more instructive.

Metaphor design and delivery is an art, and having an ample supply of engaging stories in your repertoire that can speak to common themes of therapy is helpful preparation. Here's another tip: *Collect great stories and keep them handy.* When you see events on the news or you observe spontaneous interactions in everyday living that illustrate well some point that you know will come up sometime with someone, write that story up and file it in a metaphor file so you can find it when you need it. This will certainly take the pressure off when you need good metaphors on some theme and nothing spontaneously leaps to mind.

Tip #64 The more specific your post-hypnotic suggestions, the more effective they're likely to be.

The state-specific responses people generate during hypnosis (such as age regression or analgesia) will typically dissipate upon emerging from hypnosis. A vehicle is generally needed for helping the client generalize results obtained during the session to other contexts. The post-hypnotic suggestion (PHS) is that vehicle. It has the bare-bones generic structure, "Later, when you're in situation ABC, you can do or experience XYZ." For example, when someone is preparing to take some important examination, doing a hypnosis session that offers suggestions for lowered anxiety, better attention to the material to be learned, and easier recall of that material may all be helpful. Then, a PHS such as, "Next week, when you're taking the exam, you can be pleased to discover how relaxed you are and how easily you can remember the material you've studied," can associate good test performance to the context of taking the exam.

The PHS can range from general to specific. Many people who studied a more traditional model of hypnosis learned to offer the general PHS attributed to the French psychologist and pharmacist Émile Coué. At the turn of the 20th century, he was a popular figure in the field of self-improvement who gave people this optimistic self-suggestion to practice: "Every day, in every way, I am getting better and better." Although this is a positive self-suggestion, it doesn't really pass the reality test. *Some* things may get better, of course, but "every day in every way?" All you have to do is catch a cold to invalidate that suggestion!

As a clinician, your suggestions have to be realistic enough and detailed enough to first be *acceptable* and then *useful* to the client. When you're trying to teach a new skill or introduce a more helpful perspective to the client, generalities may invite *some* clients to fill in the gaps with their own useful insights but are more likely to just frustrate the client who knows he or she needs to do *something* but doesn't know exactly what. Thus, the more specific your PHS, the stronger the link or association you're establishing between a particular context (or type of context) and a specific suggested response that can be more effective than what the client had previously been doing.

Tip #65 Re-alerting is a gradual process.

The same care that goes into guiding people *into* hypnosis is necessary when guiding them *out* of hypnosis. And, just as the immersion in hypnosis is a gradual one, the disengagement from hypnosis is also a gradual one. One of the most common complaints clients will have is that the suggestions given by the clinician for coming out of hypnosis were too abrupt. The client is absorbed in the experience of hypnosis, feeling good and relaxed and heard and respected and cared for, and all those other good feelings, too, and then they're seemingly suddenly told to end the experience.

You can appreciate why some clients aren't quick to end the hypnotic experience; can you imagine how good it must feel to be out of pain during hypnosis when pain has been debilitating for much too long? Or how good it must feel when you've been steeped in hopelessness and despair and now you have a new and welcome feeling of hopefulness? This is why some clients will take quite awhile to disengage from hypnosis. This is also a basis for the common myth that you can get "stuck" in hypnosis. When clients don't re-alert right away, they aren't "stuck" in hypnosis. They're still processing or just enjoying the experience and just don't want it to end yet.

It's good to remind clients that they can go back and re-experience hypnosis any time they want to with self-hypnosis skills you teach and by listening to the recording of the session again whenever they care to. Before you end a session, give the person some warning ("In just a little while you can start to bring this experience to a comfortable close") and give them some time to get closure ("Before you bring this session to an end you can take the time you want or need to absorb what's helpful to you and reach a comfortable sense of closure"). Instead of a demand ("One, two, three, open your eyes"), you can give clients the time they need ("Take your time and when you're ready, you can re-orient fully and open your eyes").

If for whatever reason a client doesn't re-orient in a timely way, you know what to do: check in and ask *neutrally* (i.e., without interpreting or presupposing its meaning) about his or her experience and then either utilize the client's response to do further work if necessary or else suggest alerting again but in a more directive way that includes whatever reassurances might be helpful. Once clients have opened their eyes, don't assume they are now out of hypnosis. There's a period of time afterwards where clients are not yet fully re-oriented, so go slowly and deliberately and engage with them to make sure they are fully alert and safe to go before you let them leave.

Tip #66 Debrief sessions, if not right away, then at the next meeting.

Once clients have emerged from hypnosis, there is the opportunity to speak to them about their experiences during the hypnosis session. The debriefing is an important opportunity to reinforce key insights and learnings shared during the hypnosis session and to also get client feedback that might suggest a change in approach for future sessions. It is a matter of clinical judgment as to how much debriefing is enough and how much is too much. Too little debriefing and you miss the chance to reinforce some of your session's key points. Too much debriefing and you subject an experiential process to a rational analysis that can rob it of its subjective value. If you decide that you'd prefer not to pick the session apart, at least not immediately, then you can delay the discussion to the next meeting, giving the client the interim period to absorb and integrate your suggestions.

In particular, when dealing with clients who are more cerebral and less inclined to give much thought or reaction to the "merely" subjective, this delay can be a good ally in getting the client to begin to value and explore their subjective experience more. Other clients may emerge from hypnosis feeling inspired, quietly reflective, excited, even "transformed." Such clients may want to dive right into talking about and sharing their experience and will not take kindly to any delay in debriefing. So, as always, you have to take the client's style and preferences into account in deciding your next move.

Some clients will ask you directly, "What was the meaning of that story you told me during hypnosis?" Again, you have to make a decision about how to best respond. If your client is someone who is thoughtful and proactive in general, then answering his or her question directly is a reasonable thing to do. But, if the client is not thoughtful or proactive and simply wants to be spoon-fed answers without having to do any thinking or planning, then you might want to delay answering ("I told you that story for a reason and there's a lot to think about, so I hope you'll use this week to give it some careful thought so we can discuss it in our next meeting"). Whether right now or not until next time, I think it's important to discuss the session's intentions and outcomes in a collaborative fashion with the client. While there may be some who would disagree, I think that telling a client, "I tell the stories but I don't explain them" is much too close to the arrogant (and childish) stance, "I know something you don't know!" It's not a respectful, therapeutic stance to take. Given the importance of the debriefing, there's good reason once again to define the interaction as a collaborative and empowering one.

One Last Tip…

The field of hypnosis is an exciting and dynamic field, one that is still growing as we continue to learn more about the hidden potentials of the mind. Keeping up with the hypnosis research and the clinical insights it yields is one of the many challenges of being a clinician. Conducting hypnosis sessions will always be more about art than science, the art of weaving together the colorful threads of ideas, perspectives, advice, inspiration, and experience into something the client can wear in all kinds of weather. As much as the artistry of hypnosis matters, though, so does the science. The scientific research of hypnosis generates new insights and gives us a chance to re-define ourselves as practitioners. We can move on from the archaic language and the myths of the "old" hypnosis to a more modern and clinically useful perspective, but only when we are willing to challenge ourselves to keep growing. That requires us to consider that, perhaps, what we thought we knew to be true really isn't and needs some revision.

I am dedicated to and passionate about advancing the field of clinical hypnosis. Despite my enthusiasm, though, far too many people still hold terribly misinformed views about hypnosis. My final tip, then, is to do all you can to inform people about the merits of hypnosis and all it has to offer in peoples' quests to improve their physical and mental health, relationships, and the quality of their lives.

Suggested Readings and Additional Resources

I have placed on my website, **www.yapko.com**, a list of books and articles that I highly recommend as additional resources for helping you take your practice of clinical hypnosis to the next level. I have also provided links to other websites that true hypnosis aficionados will find enlightening and enjoyable to visit.

I decided to place these on my website instead of in the back of this book as tradition would dictate because the lists are fluid, changing as new materials get added. When you get to the website home page, go to the 'Store' or 'Products' link and choose 'Books', then choose *Taking Hypnosis to the Next Level.*

While you're on the home page, be sure to sign up for my free electronic newsletter sharing current research, opinion pieces, book reviews, conference announcements, training opportunities, and more.

About Michael D. Yapko, Ph.D.

Michael D. Yapko, Ph.D., is a clinical psychologist and marriage and family therapist residing near San Diego California. Dr. Yapko has distinguished himself in the fields of psychotherapy and clinical hypnosis in a number of ways. Here are just a few of them:

- He is the only person in the field as of this writing to have *ever* received each of these highest awards of recognition from within the profession: the American Psychological Association *"Division 30 Award for Distinguished Contributions to Professional Hypnosis,"* the International Society of Hypnosis Lifetime Achievement *"Pierre Janet Award for Clinical Excellence,"* the American Society of Clinical Hypnosis *Presidential Award* and *Award of Merit*, and The Milton H. Erickson Foundation *"Lifetime Achievement Award For Outstanding Contributions to the Field of Psychotherapy."*

- He is the author of the leading hypnosis text in the field, a comprehensive volume called *Trancework: An Introduction to the Practice of Clinical Hypnosis*, now in its fourth edition. An updated fifth edition is in progress as of this writing.

- He has been providing keynote addresses and teaching some of the most highly rated workshops at national and international professional conferences for more than 35 years. He has conducted clinical trainings in more than 30 countries across six continents as well as all over the United States. His perspective is cross-national and multi-cultural.

- He is a clear and engaging presenter integrating current research findings with practical clinical applications. He has been described as scientifically informed and humanistically inclined.

- His depth and breadth of knowledge about hypnosis is evident in his writings and teachings. Beyond the previous 15 books and dozens of book chapters and journal articles he authored, he also wrote the authoritative sections on hypnosis, brief therapy, and treating depression for the *Encyclopedia Britannica Medical and Health Annual.*

- For further information about Dr. Yapko, including his comprehensive training programs in clinical hypnosis, please visit **www.yapko.com**

CPSIA information can be obtained
at www.ICGtesting.com
Printed in the USA
FSOW04n0219201017
39973FS

9 780991 079650